TUSCANY

ASSISI

written and researched by Hope Caton

www.purpleguide.com

The Purple Guide: Tuscany & Assisi

Credits
Writer: Hope Caton
Editor: Robin Bell
Design: Sharon Platt
Production: Dennis Platt
Cartography: Anderson Geographics Ltd
Additional research: Les Lester, Diana Gordon-Smith
Web site design: Mark Parker at Escape Media **www.escape-media.com**
Photography: All photographs by Hope Caton, except pages 21,40,59,64,76
by Bruce Gordon-Smith, and page 175 by Sharon Platt
Cover images: (front) John Heseltine/Italian Archive, (back) Hope Caton

Publishing Information
Published in the United Kingdom in March 2004 by:
The Purple Guide Ltd
Teddington Studios
Broom Road
Teddington Middlesex
TW11 9NT

ISBN 0-9547234-0-6
Printed in The Netherlands by Chevalier
Maps © 2004 Anderson Geographics Ltd. Used by permission.

Sales
The Purple Guide can be purchased in larger quantities at discounted prices
for use in promotions or as premiums. We are also able to supply custom cover
branding. For information, telephone our sales department on 020 8614 2277
or email: **info@purpleguide.com**

Write to Us
We welcome the views and suggestions of our readers. If we include your
contribution in our next edition, we will send you a copy of the book, or any other
Purple Guide that you would prefer.
Please write to us at the address above or email: **feedback@purpleguide.com**

The publishers have done their best to ensure that the information found in
The Purple Guide: Tuscany & Assisi is current and accurate. Some information
may be liable to change. The publishers cannot accept responsibility for any loss,
injury or inconvenience that may result from the use of this book.

From the Author	4
Welcome to *Tuscany & Assisi*	5
The Italians	6
Tuscany	8
Florence	16
Siena	80
San Gimignano	94
Lucca	100
Tuscan Towns	112
Lake Trasimeno	126
Pisa	128
Tuscany Coast	140
Assisi	158
Food & Wine	170
Shopping	204
Travel Basics	216
Index	234
Recommended Reading	238

Maps

Tuscany and Umbria	14-15
Florence	78-79
Siena	92-93
Lucca	110-111
Pisa	138-139

CONTENTS

About the Author
Hope Caton moved to London from Canada in 1997. It wasn't long before she was writing scripts and storylines for television. Hope found her true profession when she was offered a contract to develop and write a guidebook programme for a major tour operator. She has a Fine Arts degree in photography, a talent for writing and a passion for travel.
Now she writes for The Purple Guide.

From the Author

The stories and information included in this book are personal choices of mine. All the history and practical information has been researched and verified but not everything about Tuscany has been included. When I travel I don't have time to see everything and, I believe, neither do you. A person on holiday wants to have fun, perhaps learn some history, and pick up an anecdote or two to share with friends over dinner.

I've seen many beautiful places and Tuscany is still my favourite destination. As an artist, I dreamed of Florence for years before I finally made the trip. It did not disappoint. When one looks at the history of art, there are specific periods when many artists gathered together in one place and time. They became friends and enemies, inspired and challenged each other to push further, do better work, achieve greatness. Florence during the Renaissance was such a place. But lest we get carried away with reverence, we must remember that these artists were people. They liked to drink, enjoyed sex, and lived real lives. It is the stories of these lives that interest me: the stories of the underdog, the stories of the saints.

Tuscany is home to great food and wine. I enjoy cooking, especially Italian dishes, and prefer restaurants that offer a personal touch. I've endeavoured to include some in all price ranges and across all regions of Tuscany. The best of these are family owned so the list is weighted in favour of small, local establishments. Wine tours are great fun but require advance booking; I've included websites where possible to help you make the arrangements. For those in self-catering accommodation, you will find food and wine shops in the shopping section. I love a bargain, so I've made sure to list all the designer outlets around Florence.

When I travel I walk everywhere with a camera around my neck and a bag slung over my shoulder. I've kept this book light and compact because I don't like carrying a heavy guidebook. Sharon, our designer, has used a larger font: she doesn't think people should have to wear reading glasses to read their guidebook. Good maps are important: our cartographer, James, has been making maps for 15 years. Accuracy is essential and I'd like to thank Robin, our editor, for organising my thoughts and ideas and forcing me to check the facts, again.

Welcome to *Tuscany & Assisi*

The British love affair with Italy has been going on for over four centuries and shows no signs of abating. Over two million Britons visit every year, and 350,000 of them find their way to Tuscany. This is a region that demands a return visit: once is never enough.

How do we explain this passion? The combination of a beautiful landscape, splendid wines and world-famous cuisine are important. Those who love art and all things from the Renaissance will find their heart's desire. The abundance of sunshine in the seasons where it matters will always appeal to those from northern climates.

But there's more: unlike some European destinations, local charm has not been ruined by over-development. Town centres retain their unique character: the Italian love of beauty – and their laws – demand it. Variety in the Tuscan landscape means there is something for everyone here: Alpine peaks in the north soar to 2,000 metres; sandy beaches are waiting on the coast; the undulating hills of central Tuscany, lined by rows of dark green cypresses, provide peaceful vistas that have inspired artists and visitors for centuries. In summer, there is a local festival nearly every day.

The British love of things Italian continues, and The Purple Guide is offered as our contribution to this passion. We hope that you find it useful, practical, attractive to look at, and above all, enjoyable to read.

The Italians

Italians love to have fun. They love to talk, laugh, argue and be loud. Morning commuter trains are not quiet places where passengers sit silently behind their morning papers, Italian trains are alive with the sound and bustle of human voices. Italians don't queue, as they consider it to be a charming British custom.

Passeggiata is the time-honoured ritual that demonstrates Italians' love of being social: friends meet up without appointment for all know that in the late afternoon the entire community will go out for a walk. It is a time to show off the new baby, walk beside the boy you fancy or discuss recent health problems with the local wise woman. Time spent enjoying life and being together.

In Catholicism there are many saints who have a day dedicated to their name. This suits even the secular Italian as it results in more time off to have fun. A saint's day is another excuse to have a festival in a season full of feast days and celebrations. Unfortunately, this can result in museums and monuments being closed just on the day you have planned a visit. The work/life balance differs from the north to the south of Italy, with the work ethic stronger in the north. This has been a cause for suspicion: southern Italians think the northerners are really German and northerners consider that southerners are Greek.

Three ingredients are necessary for an Italian's enjoyment of life: beauty, food and family. It could be argued that Italian culture is visual in much the same way that the UK has a literary culture. Italian students will hotly debate the merits of this painter over that sculptor in much the same way English students debate the merits of Shakespeare over Marlowe.

Beauty is not a luxury for Italians, it is essential to the appreciation of life itself, an aesthetic that produces some of the best fashion and industrial designers in the world.

However, this also means that there is social pressure to take care over one's appearance and a strong emphasis is placed on health, diet and food. Italians can talk for hours about this or that medical or elimination problem. People take notice of each other: the shoes, the cut of the suit, the fabric. During the second world war, Italy was the only country where every escaped allied soldier was captured. No matter how they tried, the escapees were unable to blend in with the locals. Italians aren't fooled.

Food is key to a good life and must be prepared and eaten according to strict principles. The ingredients should be acquired locally, must be absolutely fresh, ideally home-grown in a garden or purchased at the market in the morning. For the best meals, ask your waiter what is fresh on the day. *Che cosa avete oggi?*

Family is at the heart of Italian life yet the country has the lowest birth rate in Europe. Women's attitudes are changing and they want more freedom to establish careers and determine their own futures outside the security of marriage. However, the mother-son bond remains strong and it is compulsory for couples to eat Sunday lunch with Mama, whether they are married or not. Single men of all ages will bring along the week's laundry to be lovingly washed and ironed. It is not uncommon for family members to live together in the same town or village for generations.

In the Renaissance, Italy was controlled by powerful families: the Medici, the Borghese, the Orsini. Names have changed but dynastic families represent the ruling elite: Berlusconi, Agnelli, Ferragamo. Versace continues in spite of Gianni's murder; Donatella works to build up the company she will hand over to her daughter, Gianni's niece and heir. The word nepotism derives from *il nipote*, which is the Italian word for grandson, cousin and/or nephew.

TUSCANY

POPPIES NEAR SIENA

Introducing Tuscany

The word Tuscany brings three things to mind: art, food and wine. Add sun, cypress trees, hilltop towns, friendly people and you have what some consider paradise on earth. This is the birthplace of the Renaissance, and the source of inspiration for chefs all over the world.

The modern name Tuscany, or *Toscana*, comes from the Latin *Etrusci,* shortened to *Tusci.* The origins of the Etruscan civilisation remain a mystery because there are no written records. Their language has not been fully deciphered, partly because its roots are not wholly Indo-European as are those of Latin. Some historians suspect that the Minoans of Crete may have escaped to Etruria after an earthquake destroyed their culture.

The Etruscans were Italy's first major civilisation, with artifacts dating from 800 BC. They were an artistic people who loved to eat and drink. Carvings on Etruscan sarcophagi often depict buxom women and banquet tables loaded with food and wine. They were early masters in the art of bronze casting: their land was a rich source of copper and tin (from which bronze is made) as well as lead and iron ore.

Mineral wealth, combined with the engineering skills for building roads and draining land, meant that this was an advanced civilisation capable of producing great works of art. Possibly the earliest named sculptor in Italy is an Etruscan named Vulca, who worked in *Veii* (Lazio) and is known for his terra-cotta *Apollo.*

The Roman republic was established in 509 BC, when the last Etruscan king was expelled from Rome. Tuscany was absorbed into the Empire.

After the demise of the Western Empire in the 5th century AD, Germanic tribes controlled the region, with the Lombards ruling from 568 to 774.

The Feud

The history of Tuscany is a story of rivalry, revenge and ambition. In 754 AD Pope Stephen II called on the help of the French to oust the Lombards. Charlemagne was successful, conquering all of Italy in two years. As a reward he was crowned the first Holy Roman Emperor by Pope Leo III in 800 AD. But, the seeds of rivalry were planted: by establishing an alternative to papal authority, forces began to ally on either side.

A struggle began between the papacy and the Holy Roman Empire, with families joining two rival factions: the Guelph and the Ghibelline. Guelphs were supporters of the papacy, while Ghibellines supported the Emperor. Passions were inflamed when Pope Gregory IX excommunicated the Holy Roman Emperor Frederick II in 1228. Battles continued to be fought throughout the 13th and 14th centuries. Tuscan hilltop towns such as San Gimignano are the legacy of this medieval conflict.

There was also a power struggle between the new middle class of merchants and artisans, allied with the Guelphs, and the old feudal aristocracy seeking to retain the status quo of the Emperor's Ghibelline faction.

The feud engulfed all of Tuscany and Umbria. Siena and Arezzo were Ghibelline while Florence and San Gimignano supported the Guelphs. In Umbria the Ghibelline Assisi attacked Guelph Perugia. A young soldier named Francis had his first vision in a Perugia jail. He is now the Patron Saint of Italy.

Ultimately, the real winners of the conflict were the Medici, who established a ruling dynasty in the power vacuum left by the feud. They began as bankers, but through shrewd marriages and alliances the Medici became popes, the first being Leo X. The Duchy of Tuscany was established by the Medici so that they might become dukes and noblemen with proper titles.

The Renaissance

From the French word for 'rebirth', this period in European history is usually considered to have begun in Italy in the 14th century. Florence is widely regarded as the birthplace of the Renaissance. By this time it was home to a prosperous wool and textile industry. There were 72 arts and crafts guilds in Tuscany that were patrons of art and architecture. Their wealth, combined with the church and that of several families (including the Medici), funded Renaissance art.

It became fashionable for wealthy families to commission a frescoed chapel, resulting in competition for the best artists. Churches would also compete: artists required dead bodies for anatomical study, so access to cadavers was often used to entice artists such as Michelangelo to work for the church.

The resources of the Tuscan land contributed to Renaissance art and architecture. As well as copper and tin for bronze, there was the extraordinary white marble from Carrara, used for building as well as for sculpture.

The Tuscan legacy to the arts is exceptional. Visitors today can enjoy works by Giotto, Donatello, Masaccio, da Vinci, Michelangelo and Botticelli, all within a 15 minute walk from the Piazza della Signoria in Florence. Visit a church in any Tuscan town and you will see frescoes and sculptures created by great artists.

Modern Times

Every Tuscan city has its own special flavour and atmosphere. The ordered tidiness of Siena explodes into chaos twice every summer with the running of the *Palio* (story p 84). Pisa was once a great maritime power and is now a university town with a vibrant night life. Viareggio and Forte dei Marmi are examples of seaside towns built in the *Liberty* (Art Deco) style, with Forte dei Marmi being the place to go for celebrity-watching.

Lucca is completely flat and is based on a Roman street plan. Beware of the bicycles! Arezzo, one of Tuscany's wealthiest cities, is the capital and the birthplace of Michelangelo. Here a thriving jewellery industry exists, along with a monthly antiques market. Cortona has a renowned antiques fair in September but you must be prepared to climb the steepest streets in Tuscany. Leonardo was born in Vinci, which has a museum dedicated to his machines and inventions.

Across the border in Umbria is Assisi, home of Italy's patron saint, Francis. When hilltop towns and the heat become too much for you, cool off with a boat trip around Lake Trasimeno.

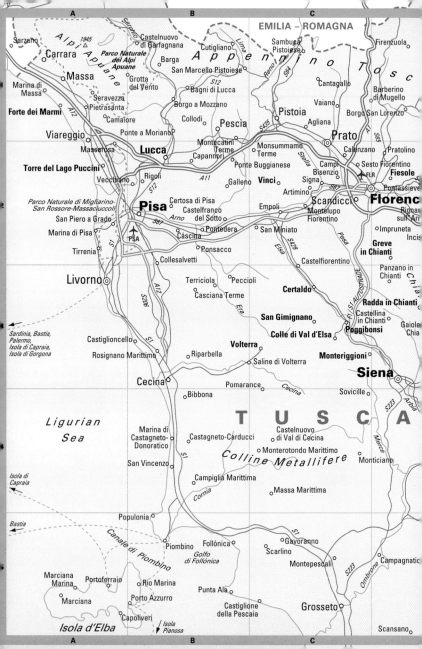

Introducing Florence

Florence emerged from the Dark Ages as a city known for its trade in wool and textiles. The river Arno provided water for washing and treating wool, and it was a source of energy for water-powered mills. By the 13th century, Florence was one of Italy's leading powers: a wealthy city backed by a powerful banking sector, ready to fund the Renaissance.

The gold *Florin* became a standard currency in medieval Europe. The coin was stamped on one side with the city's symbol, the lily, and on the other with the city's patron saint, John the Baptist. Dressed in his costume of skins and alongside the symbol of the Lamb, he seems an appropriate protector for a city founded on a highly lucrative wool trade.

The historical centre is compact: it's easy to walk to the many museums, palaces and galleries, which are the legacy of the city's importance during the Renaissance. Giotto, Donatello, Masaccio, Brunelleschi, Ghiberti, Michelangelo, da Vinci and Botticelli all lived in Florence and their works adorn the city.

David stands proudly in three locations: atop the Piazzale Michelangelo looking towards the city, in the Piazza Signoria watching over the tourists, and in the Accademia where the original sculpture resides.

Walking between the various cultural attractions will mean crossing the Piazza Signoria several times per day. Here is the heart of Florence: in this outdoor sculpture gallery *David* stands alongside the works of Donatello, Bandinelli, Cellini and Giambologna's *Rape of the Sabine*.

Renaissance architecture favoured clean, elegant buildings in an unbroken façade which can at times feel oppressive. Sounds of scooters reverberating off the masonry can be disconcerting, but you are never far from a restful piazza.

WHEN CROSSING THE STREET IT IS ADVISABLE TO WALK AT A STEADY PACE. FLORENTINE MOTORCYCLISTS WILL JUDGE YOUR WALKING SPEED AND DRIVE AROUND YOU RATHER THAN COME TO A FULL STOP.

In the Second World War, Florence declared itself neutral in an effort to protect its valuable art and architectural treasures. A 900 metre *respected area* was decreed around the Ponte Vecchio. Monuments and treasures were protected with wooden cages and sandbags; the most precious were removed to the countryside.

The Allies advanced up the peninsula and in August 1944 they entered at Porta Romana, south of the Arno. The Germans retreated north of the river and an order was given to blow up all bridges. Thankfully, Field Marshal Kesselring decreed that the Ponte Vecchio was not to be mined. The Germans retreated northward as the English flag flew over the Pitti palace.

Considerably more damage to priceless artworks was caused by the terrible flood of 1966. Torrential rainfall over the 3rd and 4th November increased the level of the Arno to 11 metres which then overflowed with water and a thick, sticky mud. Artworks were damaged at Santa Croce, the Duomo and the Baptistry.

Modern Florence is known for leather goods. Here another ancient Italian tradition survives: just as wealthy families once wielded enormous power and influence over every area of Florentine life, the Ferragamo family have amassed a large fortune through their designer shoe and leather goods label. They have recently expanded into hotels, sailing yachts and wine.

Piazza della Signoria

The piazza takes its name from the Priors (*Signoria*), who ruled Florence during the time of the Republic. Facing the piazza is the Palazzo Vecchio, begun in 1299. Here the Priors lived out their two-month term of office in a quasi-monastical way, cloistered together for the duration. Priors were chosen from members of guilds fundamental to the prosperity of Florence: the *Cambio* (bankers); *Calimala* (textile importers); and the *Lana* (wool manufacturers). The Lana were the most prominent guild. Much of their wealth coming from their complete control of all the branches of the wool industry.

As the political centre of Florence, the Piazza is where Cosimo Medici (story p 50) was arrested. But before being exiled he gave a speech, reminding soldiers how often he had personally paid their wages. He returned quietly, at dawn, a year later in 1434.

Girolamo Savonarola (story p 58) was burned at the stake in the piazza in 1498, the same year that Niccolo Machiavelli became secretary to the Council of Florence.

Streets lead from the Piazza della Signoria to the Uffizi Gallery, the Bargello, Santa Croce and the Duomo. The Ponte Vecchio is nearby, leading to the Palazzo Pitti. Most of Florence's cultural attractions are within a 15 minute walk from the Piazza della Signoria.

In the Loggia dei Lanzi, where people often sit and rest, you will find sculptures by Cellini and Giambologna. Beggars are common here, especially in summer.

CARRY SMALL CHANGE WITH YOU IN ORDER THAT YOU MAY GIVE A FEW PENNIES AWAY IF A BEGGAR BECOMES AGGRESSIVE. NEVER SHOW A BEGGAR YOUR WALLET.

If this is your first glimpse of David, you are looking at a copy. The original is in the Accademia. Beside the Palazzo Vecchio, in *Via de Gondi*, is a leather market.

Palazzo Vecchio

055 276 8325
09.00-19.00 Monday - Saturday
09.00-13.00 Sunday & Thursday
closed on public holidays
map E3

The Palazzo continues to function as a town hall and political centre of Florence. Officials haven't lived here since the Medici moved to Pitti palace in 1550.

The paintings in the *Salone dei Cinquento* are by Vasari, but imagine what might have been: Both Leonardo da Vinci and Michelangelo were commissioned to fresco battle scenes on opposite walls. Leonardo was to paint the *Battle of Anghiari,* Michelangelo, the *Battle of Cascina.*

The artists hated each other. The rivalry came to be known as the '*Battle of the Battles*'. Leonardo was jealous of the Medici's patronage of Michelangelo, who in turn despised Leonardo for his illegitimacy. Work was never completed as both artists were summoned elsewhere: Michelangelo to Rome, Leonardo to Milan.

PALAZZO VECCHIO

Murder on the Bridge

In *The Florentine Histories*, Niccolo Machiavelli writes of
the death of the young Buondelmonte in 1216, which
ignited the feud between the Guelphs and Ghibellines:

*The most powerful Florentine families were the
Buondelmonti and the Uberti, and after them the Amidei
and the Donati. Among the Donati was a rich widow
who planned to marry her beautiful daughter to the
young Buondelmonte. She had not told anyone her plan.*

*She discovered that he had become engaged to a
daughter of the Amidei. She still hoped that her daughter's
beauty would be enough to end the betrothal before the
wedding. Buondelmonte was passing her house and she
went out to congratulate him on the wife he had chosen,
adding that she had been keeping her daughter just for
him. She opened her door a little way to allow him to set
eyes on the girl.*

*Buondelmonte was overcome by her beauty and, seeing
that she was as well-born as his betrothed, was filled with
such passion that he answered, mindless of the promises
he had made, the insult and implications of his action:
'Then you have been keeping her for me, and I would
indeed be ungrateful if I failed to accept your offer while
there is still time'. Without any further delay he married
her.*

*The news filled the Amadei family, and their allies the
Umberti, with wrath. In a meeting with elders from both
families it was resolved that such action required
vengeance: Buondelmonte's death.*

*On Easter day, four assassins waited in the house of
Amadei on the Ponte Vecchio. Buondelmonte, obviously
thinking it was as easy to forget a grievance as to break off
an engagement, was crossing the bridge mounted on a
white horse when he was attacked and murdered close to a
statue of Mars.*

Il Ponte Vecchio

Also called *The Old Bridge* or the *Bridge of Gold* because of its age and the quaint jewellers' shops on either side. Until 1218 it was the only bridge that crossed the River Arno. It was reconstructed by Taddeo Gaddi after a flood in 1345.

The bridge is famous for the gold shops and medieval houses which overhang the river. Following the Florentine tradition of gold-working which became famous in the 15th century, jewellers still trade here.

Above the shops on the left-hand side you can see the Vasari Corridor, built as a covered walkway to connect Palazzo Vecchio to the Ponte Vecchio and the Pitti Palace. This enabled the Medicis to travel discreetly between the city centre and their home, thus avoiding contact with disgruntled citizens.

GUIDED VISITS ARE AVAILABLE BY REQUEST. BOOKINGS SHOULD BE MADE WELL IN ADVANCE.
TELEPHONE: 055 265 4321

PONTE VECCHIO

Dante

Dante Alighieri (1265-1321) was born in Florence, the son of a lawyer. His stature in Italian literature is similar to that of Shakespeare in English. Dante's most important work is the *Divine Comedy*, a journey through hell, purgatory and heaven, written in three parts: *Inferno, Purgatorio* and *Paradiso*.

Beatrice Portinari was the symbol of female perfection in Dante's works. Though they met only a few times and rarely spoke, her beauty inspired him. She appears as an angel in *Purgatorio* and guides him upwards to Paradise, where they ultimately gaze upon the perfection of God.

Dante's wife was Gemma Donati of the Guelph faction. Dante fought on their side at the battle of Campalidon in 1289, when the Ghibellines were defeated. He became a Prior in 1300. As a member of the White Guelphs, he was fighting to make Florence independent of popes, emperors and foreigners. He was exiled in 1302 when the Black Guelphs, loyal to the pope, defeated and banished the White Guelphs.

Dante never returned to Florence; he wrote the Divine Comedy in exile. He is buried in Ravenna which has always refused Florentine requests to have his bones returned. Instead there is a monument outside the Santa Croce church. A small museum, (Casa di Dante, p 62) is dedicated to him in the house of his birth on Via Santa Margherita.

In the Inferno, Dante questions his friend Ciacco about the future of Florence. Ciacco replies:

> *Two men are just, but are not listened to there;*
> *Pride, Envy and Avarice are the three sparks*
> *that have set the hearts of all on fire.*

Giotto

Giotto di Bondone (1266-1337) was born in Colle de Vespignano in 1267, the son of a farmer. Legend has it that at the age of ten, Giotto was looking after sheep and drawing one of them on a rock with a flat stone. The great painter, Cimabue, passed by. He was so impressed with the boy's ability he immediately took him into his workshop. A more likely story is that Giotto was apprenticed to a wool merchant, but spent so much time at Cimabue's workshop that he was finally allowed to study painting.

Realism was Giotto's chief gift to painting. One day he painted a fly on the nose of a figure Cimabue had been painting. The master returned several times to brush the fly away, so realistically was it drawn.

Considered the first Renaissance painter, Giotto was the first artist to depict spiritual and supernatural subjects in warm, human, earthly terms. The *Ognissanti Madonna* altarpiece, now in the Uffizi, was the first to show the Madonna as a woman with breasts. In earlier painting, particularly Byzantine, the Madonna was represented as the austere queen of heaven.

Giotto's crucifix for the church of Santa Maria Novella (p 60) shows the facial features relaxed with lips parted, hands and body drawn with accurate anatomical detail. Blood spurts from Christ's wounds and runs down his side to his knee, a depiction that would be copied for centuries.

Giotto had a large workshop and many of the most famous artists of the Renaissance were apprenticed to him. He designed the *Campanile* (Bell Tower) of the Duomo in 1334.

Dante and Giotto knew each other: Giotto painted Dante and Dante mentioned Giotto in his writings.

Santa Maria del Fiore

Called the Duomo because of its magnificent dome, the cathedral is the most prominent building in Florence. This is Europe's fourth largest church.

The Piazza del Duomo contains the Cathedral (Duomo), Baptistry and Bell Tower (Campanile). Art and artifacts from the Duomo and Baptistry are to be found in the Museo dell'Opera del Duomo near the corner of Via dell'Orivolo. Be sure not to miss this museum located behind the cathedral.

The neo-Gothic cathedral façade, designed to match Giotto's Campanile, was added in 1887.

As well as being a tourist attraction, the interior of the Duomo is still used for daily mass by visitors and Florentines alike.

The Dome

The grand dome, designed by Brunelleschi, rises to a height of 330 feet. There are 436 steps to the top. The stairway follows a labyrinth of corridors and spiral steps up to the lantern at the top of the dome. From this height you can see the spectacular sights of the city and the surrounding Tuscan countryside. A closer look at the inside of the dome and its ornate decoration is also possible whilst climbing to the top. Not for those who are prone to vertigo but well worth the climb.

Inside the Duomo

The stained glass window is often overlooked by visitors to the Duomo. It depicts *The Resurrection of Christ* by Paolo Uccello, who also made the statue *Sir John Hawkwood on a Horse*. Sir John was a mercenary from Essex who was alternately protecting and attacking Florence during the time of the Republic in the 1400s.

Museo dell Opera del Duomo

09.00–18.50 Monday-Saturday, April-October
09.00–17.20 Monday-Saturday, November-March
map E2

This museum displays art works removed from the Duomo, Baptistry and Campanile in order to preserve them from damage. Visit Donatello's *Mary Magdalene*, and *St John the Baptist*, Michelangelo's *Pieta*, original bronze Baptistry doors and Campanile reliefs, and Brunelleschi's model for the Dome.

The Campanile

This elegant tower was begun by Giotto in 1334 when he was appointed city architect but he died before it was completed. Andrea Pisano (of the Pisano family responsible for Pisa's *Campo dei Miracoli*, story p 134) and Francesco Talenti contributed to the project which was completed 1359. Climb 414 steps to the top for a magnificent view. The reliefs on the Campanile depict the Creation of Man, Arts and Industry and were carved by Andrea Pisano.

The Baptistry

Dating from the 4th century, this may be the oldest building in Florence. Dante was baptised here. The ceiling has a 13th century mosaic illustrating the Last Judgement. The east and north doors are by Lorenzo Ghiberti. The older, south set of doors are by Pisano.

Three doors of this building illustrate stories from the Bible in bronze. They are copies, as the flood of 1966 caused considerable damage. Now restored, the original bronze doors are in the Museo dell'Opera del Duomo.

The east doors were commissioned in 1401 to mark the city's deliverance from the plague. Trial panels made by Ghiberto and Brunelleschi are regarded by some as the first works of the Renaissance. The use of perspective and the individuality of the figures are completely different from Florentine Gothic art.

The east door panels illustrate the following stories:

1. *Adam and Eve are expelled from Eden*
2. *Cain murders his brother Abel*
3. *The drunkenness of Noah and his sacrifice*
4. *Abraham and the sacrifice of Isaac*
5. *Jacob and Esau*
6. *Joseph sold into slavery*
7. *Moses receiving the ten commandments*
8. *The fall of Jericho*
9. *The battle with the Philistines*
10. *Solomon and the Queen of Sheba*

BAPTISTRY DOORS, JACOB & ESAU PANEL

Brunelleschi

Filippo Brunelleschi (1337-1446), along with his friend Masaccio, is credited with rediscovering the laws of scientific perspective. Famously hot-tempered, he insulted Donatello by saying his good friend had carved *'the body of a peasant on the cross'* for the Bardino di Vernis chapel in Santa Croce. To show how it should be done, he made his own crucifix for the Santa Maria Novella.

Brunelleschi was the father of Renaissance architecture. In his early twenties he left Florence for Rome, where he studied mathematics and architecture. After his return to Florence he was commissioned as the Duomo's leading artist and architect. The design for the dome was his most remarkable achievement: an inner shell meant that the dome was built in sections and without scaffolding. It was the greatest feat of its kind since ancient times.

His rival, Ghiberti, claimed that he had contributed to the cupola of the dome but never succeeded in convincing his fellow citizens. Although Ghiberti was paid, along with Brunelleschi, as *capomaestri* of the cupola, it was Brunelleschi who received the higher salary.

Florence expected every artist to do his duty to the State. Art was a skill which had other practical aspects: long before da Vinci, Brunelleschi designed engineering and hydraulic schemes for building fortifications of Tuscan towns. He was consulted in the campaign against the ancient enemy, Lucca, as an advisor in destroying the fortifications which he himself had designed.

In his later years Brunelleschi's style became more sculptural, as in the Pazzi Chapel in the Santa Croce. He is known for his graceful arches, which are evident in his design for the portico of the Spedale degli Innocenti.

Ghiberti

The *Arte della Calimala* (a textile guild) held a competition for a set of bronze doors for the north entrance of the Baptistry. Renowned artists from across Italy made submissions.

Arch rivals Lorenzo Ghiberti (1378-1455) and Filippo Brunelleschi were the two finalists. Both were young, 23 and 24, and neither had the experience to undertake the commission. The artists were required to make samples of the *Relief of the Sacrifice of Isaac*, now on display at the Bargello. It was so difficult to choose between them that they were asked to collaborate. Brunelleschi flatly refused and Ghiberti got the contract. In November 1403, he undertook to deliver at least three panels a year, with the faces, hair and trees to be produced by his own hand. It would take him 25 years to complete the first set of doors which tell the life of Christ.

The Florentines were so delighted with Ghiberti's bronze panels that they immediately commissioned another for the east entrance. Doors sculpted by Andrea Pisano were originally hung there but were moved to the south to make way for Ghiberti. It would take him another 27 years.

Michelangelo named the doors *The Gates of Paradise*. Each panel illustrates a story from the Old Testament.

Ghiberti's advances in perspective are heavily influenced by experiments made by Brunelleschi, something Ghiberti would never credit in his memoirs, *Commentaries*, in which he boasts:

'Few things of importance have been done in our land where I have not had a hand in the design or the direction'.

Masaccio

In 1423, the wealthy Felice Brancacci had just returned from Egypt where he had served as Florence's ambassador. He commissioned Masolino da Panicale to decorate his chapel in the Santa Maria Del Carmine. Masolino had also worked on the Baptistry doors while apprenticed to Ghiberti.

Masolino decided to collaborate with the young painter, Tommaso Cassai, known as Masaccio (1401-28). They began work in 1424 but after a year Masolino left for Budapest. Masaccio carried on alone until his mysterious death in Rome in 1428 when he was just 27. The cycle of frescoes was completed by Filippino Lippi.

Masaccio was friendly with Brunelleschi and Donatello and the three artists hoped for a commission that would employ all their talents. Sadly, this did not materialise. Together Masaccio and Brunelleschi experimented with perspective and developed methods still used by painters and sculptors today. Masaccio's fresco *Trinity*, in the Santa Maria Novella, was the first time that full perspective had been used. Another innovation was his use of light to define the human body.

The Brancacci chapel frescoes in the Basilica Santa Maria del Carmine are important as they illustrate emotions so forcefully. Masaccio was not interested in grace or beauty: his Apostles are rugged working men. The figures express severe torment. *Expulsion from Paradise* is a scene of tense psychological drama, with the figures uncompromising in their pain.

The entrance to the Brancacci Chapel is at the side of the Basilica Santa Maria del Carmine. (See p 60 for opening times and map reference.)

Santa Croce & Santa Maria Novella

Painting and sculpture became a way of communicating the Christian faith to people who could not read. Thus religious buildings came to be seen as great illustrated bibles. The interiors of Santa Croce and Santa Maria Novella demonstrate the importance of painting as both adornment and instruction to the faithful.

It was only the wealthy who were in a position to build or decorate a complete family chapel. Some of the prominent families of Florence were particularly active: the Bardi, the Strozzi and the Tornabuoni (uncles to the Medici) are among the faces depicted.

Fresco painting was technically difficult as it was executed on wet plaster. The artist had to work quickly, finishing the day's portion of wall before the plaster dried. Correcting mistakes was difficult: once the paint had soaked into the plaster and dried, the artist could only correct the work by painting over it. Frescoes only survive well in dry climates; many were damaged in the floods of 1966.

The Franciscan church of Santa Croce and its rival, the Dominican Santa Maria Novella, were the first churches in Florence to possess mural decoration. Artists benefited from this rivalry and often used it to their own ends: Brunelleschi sculpted his crucifix for the Gondi Chapel in Santa Maria Novella because he did not like the 'earthly' quality of Donatello's Christ in the Santa Croce.

Giotto's groundbreaking crucifix hangs in the sacristy of the Santa Maria Novella and his frescoes decorate the Bardi Chapel in Santa Croce. Ghirlandaio painted the frescoes for the Tornabuoni Chapel in the Santa Maria Novella with the help of his student, Michelangelo, whose tomb is in Santa Croce.

(See p 60 for church opening times and map reference.)

GHIRLANDAIO'S FRESCO IN THE SANTA MARIA NOVELLA

Donatello

Donatello (1386-1466) fused art and nature to make his sculpture appear to live and breathe. While he was working he was known to look at his creation and mutter, *'Speak, damn you, speak!'*. However, the bold individuality of the artist combined with the innovation of his sculpture may have combined to diminish demand for his work.

Born Donato di Niccolo di Betto Bardi, the son of a wool comber, he was apprenticed to Lorenzo Ghiberti and at the age of 17 was assisting in sculpting the bronze doors for the Duomo Baptistry. There he learned the art of casting metal later to be used with such genius in his *David*, the first free-standing bronze nude since antiquity. The unveiling caused quite a stir but the sculpture is pure Renaissance, symbolizing the ideal of physical grace and beauty.

Little is known about the commissioning of *David*. There are no references to it during Donatello's lifetime. It may have been commissioned by his patron, Cosimo de'Medici, to celebrate Florentine success in negotiating peace with Milan. Donatello had an uneasy relationship with his patron: Cosimo once gave the sculptor a set of respectable red clothes because he didn't approve of Donatello walking barefoot dressed in rags. Too independent to accept the clothing and its implications, Donatello continued to dress as he pleased.

Donatello lived to be 80 and remained unmarried. His good friends were his contemporaries Brunelleschi and the painter Masaccio. Donatello is portrayed barefoot and praying in Masaccio's fresco *St Peter Healing with his Shadow* in the Brancacci Chapel of the Santa Maria del Carmine church (p 60).

The *David* can be seen in the Bargello (p 46).

Michelangelo

Michelangelo Buonarroti (1475-1564) was born in Arezzo, the second of five brothers. His mother was too sick to nurse him, so he was placed in a family of stone cutters. He completely absorbed the craft of hammer and chisel and decided to become a sculptor. When he confessed his dream of becoming an artist, his father flew into a rage, claiming that artists were no better than shoemakers.

Artists had no social standing and their workshops tended to attract the sons of poorer families who could not afford the apprenticeship fees of the guilds. The young painter or sculptor had to find a place in the workshop of an established master and this became his home. An apprentice lived and worked under his master from four to 13 years. This was not the plan Michelangelo's father had for his son.

To prepare him for a career in business, Michelangelo was sent to Florence to study Latin. While at school he befriended a student, apprenticed to the painter Domenico Ghirlandaio, who encouraged the youth to follow his dreams. At 13, Michelangelo further enraged his father by agreeing to become an apprentice in Ghirlandaio's workshop, where he learned the art of fresco. This skill was to be fully realised later in his masterpiece at the Sistine Chapel. After two years of painting, he studied sculpture under Donatello's teacher, Bertoldo di Giovanni.

Lorenzo de'Medici spotted the boy's talent and invited him into the Medici household where he became friendly with Lorenzo's son and nephew; the future popes Leo X and Clement VII. Lorenzo died and Michelangelo was forced to flee to Bologna when the Medicis were exiled.

Michelangelo travelled to Rome where he was able to study ancient classical statues that were being unearthed. There was a trade in fake antiquities at the time and, needing money, Michelangelo carved and distressed a cupid which he sold to a Cardinal as an antique. The Cardinal spotted the forgery, but was impressed with the sculptor and commissioned an original, which was later rejected for being too sensual. The sculpture was *The Bacchus,* which now resides in the Bargello (p 46).

His next work was the *Pieta* for St Peter's Basilica in Rome. One of the world's most famous works of art, it was finished just before Michelangelo's 25th birthday. It is his only signed work. When the Pieta was unveiled, he overheard a pilgrim credit the work to Christoforo Solari, a Lombard. In a fit of rage he returned that night with hammer and chisel to carve *'Michelangelo Buonarroti, Florentine, made this'* on the sash across Mary's breast. He was later to regret this rash action, which he attributed to selfish pride.

After several years of political confusion, a Republic was once again proclaimed in Florence. Michelangelo was able to return to his beloved city. Twelve days after the proclamation of the republic, in the year 1501, the *Arte della Lana* (wool guild) commissioned him to sculpt a statue of David. He was 26 years old.

Michelangelo wrote in his diaries:

When I returned to Florence, I found myself famous. They ask me to carve a colossal David from a 19 foot block of Carrara marble – and damaged to boot! I locked myself away in a workshop behind the cathedral, hammered and chiselled at the towering block for three long years. In spite of the opposition of a committee of fellow artists, I insisted that the figure should stand before the Palazzo Vecchio, as a symbol of our Republic. I had my way. Archways were torn down, narrow streets widened…it took 40 men five days to move it. Once in place, all Florence was astounded. A civic hero, he was a warning … whoever governed Florence should govern justly and defend it bravely. Eyes watchful...the neck of a bull…hands of a killer… the body, a reservoir of energy. He stands poised to strike.

David

Florence was experiencing uncertain times and its citizens had to be alert to the threat of war and invasion. Michelangelo used David as a model of heroic courage in the face of a seemingly unbeatable foe, a giant. The young shepherd's faith in God enabled him to overcome Israel's enemies with a slingshot. This biblical hero demonstrated that inner spiritual strength can prove to be more effective than arms.

Michelangelo was devoted to Florence's Republic and he wanted each citizen to commit himself to doing his duty. He chose to represent David as an athletic, manly character, very concentrated and ready to fight.

David and Goliath

David said to Goliath, "You come against me with sword and spear and javelin, but I come against you in the name of the Lord Almighty, the God of the armies of Israel, whom you have defied. This day the Lord will hand you over to me, and I will strike you down and cut off your head. Today I will give the carcasses of the Philistine army to the birds of the air and the beasts of the earth, and the whole world will know that there is a God in Israel. All those gathered here will know that it is not by sword or spear that the Lord saves; for the battle is the Lord's, and he will give all of you into our hands."

As the giant moved closer to attack him, David ran quickly towards the battle line to meet him. Reaching into his bag and taking out a stone, he slung it and struck the Philistine on the forehead. The stone sank into his forehead, and he fell face down on the ground. So David triumphed over Goliath with a sling and a stone; without a sword in his hand he struck down the giant and killed him.

Holy Bible, 1 Samuel 17, New International Version

Galleria dell'Accademia

Via Ricasoli, 60
055 238 8609
08.30-18.50 Tuesday-Sunday
Closed Monday
Cost: €6.50
map E1

The Academy of Fine Arts was first set up as a school in 1563 to teach drawing and design techniques. It became an art gallery in 1784. Since 1873 many of Michelangelo's most important works have been displayed here, the most famous of which is the glorious *David*.

The original sculpture was put into the Academy to protect it from pollution and possible damage. A copy was put in its place in Piazza della Signoria and another in the Piazzale Michelangelo. The gallery houses works by other Florentine artists and contemporaries of Michelangelo. A collection of Renaissance musical instruments is found in a small modern interactive gallery off to the side on the ground floor.

A large rectangular room contains Michelangelo's later sculptures and opens to the rotunda and *David*. In contrast to the Bargello (p 46), sculptures here are not displayed particularly well. Michelangelo's bodies writhing to free themselves from the marble appear to be trying to escape into the beautiful garden outside the window. However, the attraction is the *David*: white Carrara marble gleaming in the light, catching the carved detail of muscle and sinew, body ready for action, eyes watchful and wary, yet full of courage.

OUTSIDE THE GALLERY IS A KIOSK SELLING LEATHER GOODS RUN BY A LONG-MARRIED COUPLE WHO MET WHILE STUDENTS AT THE ACCADEMIA. THEY SELL A LEATHER SPECTACLES CASE TO HANG ROUND YOUR NECK, AN ITEM NOT AVAILABLE OUTSIDE OF FLORENCE.

Piazzale Michelangelo

map F5

This large square is called Piazzale Michelangelo after the copy of Michelangelo's *David* in the centre, which has a perfect view over Florence and the river Arno, spread out below. A perfect spot for taking photographs of the city of Florence by night and day.

This fantastic viewing point sits on the south side of the river Arno above the city centre. By climbing uphill, passing through Porta San Nicolo, and up the steps you can reach the square in about 15 minutes on foot.

For those not wishing to climb, buses number 12 and 13 take the tree-lined road up to the top.

A taxi will cost € 7-10.

From Siena/Firenze (SI:FI) Superstrada, take the Certosa exit and follow the road to a roundabout. Take the exit marked Firenze and continue along the road for about 4km, passing through the suburb of Galluzzo.

Bear right at the traffic lights where you will see a yellow sign for Piazzale Michelangelo. Continue along this road through two more sets of lights until you reach a junction at the top of a tree-lined avenue, bear right and follow the winding road down the hill. The Piazzazale is on the left.

PARKING HERE IS FREE. HOWEVER, LESS SCRUPULOUS TYPES HAVE TRIED TO EXTORT UP TO €20.00 FROM TOURISTS.

Toilets are located underneath the west stairs.

The jewelbox church of San Miniato (p 60) is along the road on your left.

The Bargello

Via del Proconsolo, 4
055 238 8606
08.30–13.50 daily
Closed: Monthly every 1st, 3rd, & 5th Sunday; every 2nd & 4th
Monday. Also closed 1st May, Christmas Day, New Year's Day
map E3

The forbidding and impregnable exterior hides a wonderful museum; an oasis of calm and beauty. Arrive early to enjoy the collection of Donatello and Michelangelo sculptures in peaceful surroundings.

The ground floor gallery off the courtyard contains Michelangelo's sensual *Bacchus* and his powerful bust of *Brutus* amongst his other early work. The bronze *David* by Donatello is found in the former Hall of the Great Council on the first floor to the right of the courtyard stairs. Donatello also carved a stone *David* which is on display. *John the Baptist* by Desiderio da Settignano is costumed in wool as befits the symbol of Florence. The naturalistic influence of Giotto on Donatello is evident in the small bas-relief of *Madonna and Child*. This conveys a tender moment between mother and infant not previously depicted in religious sculpture. Dante is painted in a fresco by Giotto, located in the chapel.

The Bargello was begun in 1255. It was initially a town hall, later a prison. The head of the prison and police was called the *Bargello*.

The tower bell rang out to summon Florentines to battle, or in times of seige. Executions took place in the courtyard until 1786.

In 1865, the building was opened as one of Italy's first national musems.

The Pitti Palace

Piazza Pitti
055 213 440
09.00–19.00 Tuesday-Saturday; 09.00–14.00 Sunday
Closed Monday
map C5

This palace was built by the arch rival of the Medici family, Luca Pitti.

The design is attributed to Brunelleschi, although building was started after his death in 1455. Pitti died in 1472 and the palace was completed by other, lesser-known architects.

The Medici bought the palace in 1549. It became the official seat of the Medici dynasty when Duke Cosimo moved from the Palazzo Vecchio. It was given to the state by Vittorio Emmanuel III in 1919.

There is a splendid courtyard, which is considered to be a masterpiece of Florentine Mannerist architecture.

The gallery contains works by Canova, Titian, Reubens, and Raphael.

There is also a costume gallery and a silver museum with artefacts that belonged to the Medici, as well as Chinese and Japanese ceramics.

The Modern Art gallery holds works from the 18th to 20th centuries. 'Modern' is a relative term in Florence, sometimes referring to anything that happened after the Renaissance. This collection is particularly representative of the years between the two world wars.

Take a stroll through Boboli Gardens (p 64) at the rear of the palace. It is the only park in central Florence.

A porcelain gallery in Boboli Gardens contains the largest collection of Viennese china outside of Vienna.

The Uffizi

Loggiato degli Uffizi, 6
055 238 8651
08.30-18.50 Tuesday-Sunday
Closed Monday
map D4

PRE-BOOK TICKETS FOR THE UFFIZI AND THE ACCADEMIA
BY CALLING 055 294 883. PAYMENT MUST BE MADE BY CREDIT
CARD. AN ADMINISTRATION FEE IS CHARGED: THIS COSTS
MORE BUT SAVES WAITING IN A QUEUE.

The Uffizi was built between 1560 and 1580 as new
administration offices for Duke Cosimo I. It was turned
into a gallery by Cosimo's heirs to hold the extensive
Medici art treasures. The collection is one of the greatest
of the Renaissance period and ranges from early Gothic
Art through to the High Renaissance and Mannerism.
It is considered to be the first art gallery established in
Europe. The main collection is on the top floor.

ON YOUR WAY UP THE STAIRS TO THE MAIN GALLERIES ON
THE THIRD FLOOR, BE SURE TO TAKE A DETOUR (AND A
REST) ON THE SECOND FLOOR. A SIDE GALLERY EXHIBITS
DRAWINGS BY RAPHAEL, DA VINCI, BOTTICELLI AND
MICHELANGELO.

Paintings are hung in chronological order, from
Byzantine to High Renaissance art.

The gallery devoted to Botticelli is a highlight, as are the
three Leonardo da Vincis in the adjoining room. Titian's
vibrant red is a welcome relief from the monotone of
religious paintings. The fresh energy of Goya is inspiring
after rooms full of dark landscapes.

Rest from the heat at the rooftop cafe which offers a
beautiful view over Florence.

Giovanni di Bicci de Medici

The Medici family were bankers who acquired great wealth in the 13th century, probably through financing the wars of both the Guelph and the Ghibillene. Theirs is a story full of exile and return: sometimes alone, sometimes with an army. Salvestro de Medici became the first Medici to be banished in 1387. He led the common people in a revolt of the *ciompi* (small senate) and was himself later banished for brutal dictatorial policies.

The family's fortune was restored by Giovanni di Bicci de Medici (1360-1429) who became the wealthiest banker in Italy: a shrewd businessman from poor beginnings who provided his descendants with the foundation of wealth on which to build a dynasty. Giovanni negotiated advantageous marriages for his sons, Cosimo il Vecchio and his brother, Lorenzo il Vecchio, resulting in two Medici princesses becoming queens of France and their daughters being married to Philip II of Spain and England's Charles I.

Cosimo il Vecchio

Upon Giovanni's death the Medici family was consolidated into a merchant banking firm around the two brothers. They had a close, amicable relationship in a time of family rivalries. Cosimo (1389-1464) was the more political of the two while Lorenzo was more erudite. They were linked commercially and personally, both in terms of charity and as collectors. The brothers donated books to a convent and their names are displayed proudly on the tomb they built for their parents.

The Medici had rivals: the feud with the noble Albizzi family led by Rinaldo degli Albizzi broke into open antagonism in 1433. There was high drama in Florence: Cosimo was briefly imprisoned and in danger of a death sentence. There was no fighting in the streets as there was during the Ghibilline/Guelph conflict.

The Albizzi behaved nobly, fighting their case against the Medici through the *Signoria* and the courts, unstained by blood. Cosimo and his allies were sentenced to banishment for 10 years, Lorenzo for only five.

The Albizzi failed to secure victory in an expensive war with Lucca. Brunelleschi's plan to flood the countryside around Lucca proved a dismal failure. Taxes had to be raised: rich men were forced to borrow money at high interest rates. Bankruptcies occurred. Cosimo waited in comfortable exile.

Rinaldo degli Albizzi had a miserable 12 months in Florence, coping with a growing pro-Medici feeling and trying to form alliances. He resorted to arms but miscalculated when some his supporters failed to back him. The *Signoria* creaked into action and revoked the sentence of exile on the Medici.

Cosimo crept quietly back into Florence at sunset in October 1434, accompanied only by his brother, Lorenzo, and one servant. The stealth of his re-entry is an example of the way he established power by disclaiming power. Cosimo began giving large portions of his wealth to charities, after handsomely providing for himself and all his family. He amassed the largest library in Europe.

Cosimo was the Bill Gates of the Renaissance. Like Gates, the amounts given in patronage to the arts and to the poor was a confirmation of his own position as the wealthiest man in the world. The grateful recipients of his charity became loyal supporters throughout his life. His personal taste in clothing also showed the same casual lack of ostentation, similar to Gates' love of chinos and khaki. Also like Gates, he poured his wealth into building large palaces, collecting art, and providing endowments to universities.

Cosimo il Vecchio

Cosimo was a clever and established banker who absorbed the majority of the 39 Florentine banks. As well as all major Italian cities, the Medici network of banks spread throughout Europe to France, England, Geneva, Bruges, Lubeck and Cracow. But Cosimo was not content with being just a rich banker. He also dealt in cloth and dabbled in the trading of slaves and *castrati*. Wealthy clients and friends kept him assured of political power, which he was careful to exercise with discretion.

Cosimo il Vecchio had no need of political office so he was able to exercise humility when it came to titles and official power. His title of *princeps* merely meant the first citizen, or senator. He wielded authority through his family and business connections who owed him favours.

Cosimo died in 1464. He had been in power for so long that there existed a generation of Florentines who had only known government under Medici rule. And, since the years had been prosperous, Florentines were fully prepared to support his son, (Piero the Gouty, 1416-69).

Cosimo was buried very plainly in the crypt of San Lorenzo. He appears as the grey-haired king kneeling at the feet of the Virgin in Botticelli's *Adoration of the Magi*. The kneeling figure in white is his grandson, Guiliano, and the young man holding a sword on the left of the painting is his other grandson, Lorenzo the Magnificent.

Lorenzo il Magnifico

When Piero died, his son Lorenzo (grandson of Cosimo), was only 20 and ineligible to vote. However, prominent citizens duly arrived at the Medici palace to invite Lorenzo to rule over Florence. In his time, the title of 'the Magnificent' was not specific to Lorenzo. It was an honorific that applied to distinguished citizens, including Lorenzo's father and grandfather.

Lorenzo the Magnificent continues to be remembered because the golden age of the Renaissance happened under his rule. Lorenzo (1449-92) and his brother Giuliano (1453-78) considered themselves nobility and patrons of the arts. Lorenzo was himself a poet and a close friend of Michelangelo and Botticelli.

The brothers now considered themselves above the will of the people. They did not seek the support of the populace as their grandfather Cosimo il Vecchio had been careful to do. In 1478, Lorenzo and Giuliano were attacked with swords and knives during high mass in the Duomo. Giuliano died immediately but the wounded Lorenzo escaped into the sacristy, with his protectors.

The attack came to be known as the Pazzi conspiracy, organised by the Pazzi family with the aid of the Archbishop of Pisa. The Pazzi family managed to escape but the Archbishop was seized in the Palazzo della Signoria and hanged the same evening. Thus ended the only real threat to Lorenzo's power. He ruled for a further 14 years. He married Clarice Orsini, a wealthy Roman aristocrat, who gave birth to a son, Piero, named after Lorenzo's father.

The period from Cosimo's return in 1434 to the death of his grandson Lorenzo the Magnificent in 1492 was the high point of the Florentine Renaissance.

Lorenzo's hedonistic lifestyle eroded the goodwill of the people. The priest Savonarola preached against consumption and wealth. He predicted bad times to come, both for the Medicis and for Florence and his predictions came true: after Lorenzo died the Medici banks failed. Savanarola gained power and exiled Piero, henceforth nicknamed 'the unfortunate'. It was to be 18 years before the Medici returned.

Medici Popes: Leo X and Clement VII

Lorenzo the Magnificent, banker to Pope Innocent VIII, asked that his second son, Giovanni, be made a cardinal. The Pope agreed on the condition that the appointment be kept secret for three years because Giovanni was only 14. Florence was soon abuzz with the news that one their own had been granted this honour.

In exile after Lorenzo's death, the Medicis set up a power base in Rome. Lorenzo's nephew Giulio (1478-1534) entered the church, working closely with his cousin, the new Cardinal Giovanni de Medici.

After much intrigue behind the scenes and upon defeat of the French armies in Italy, Giovanni returned to Florence in 1512 at the head of an armed company courtesy of Charles V of Spain.

Cardinal Giovanni de Medici (1475-1521) became Pope Leo X, the first Medici pope, in 1513. He bestowed the Duchy of Urbino to his cousin Lorenzo II (Lorenzo the Magnificent's grandson).

Giulio then became ruler of Florence but abdicated to become Pope Clement VII. Giulio's bastard son, Allessandro, the last male descendant of Cosimo il Vecchio, became the hereditary Duke of Florence.

The Duke of Florence

Allesandro was debauched, short-tempered and, though married to the respected Duchess Margaret, Regent of the Netherlands, he enjoyed the company of many other women. On Epiphany night in 1537, he waited in bed for a woman that his cousin, Lorenzino, had procured for him. Instead it was Lorenzino who burst in, accompanied by a hired assassin. The Duke of Florence was stabbed to death. Lorenzino fled to Venice where he in turn was assassinated in the Campo San Polo.

The Medicis gathered together and moved quickly to unite at the news of Alessandro's murder. A Medici had to be found to replace Alessandro and keep the reins of power within the family. The election of Cosimo I to head of State took place within two days of Alessandro's death. Cosimo I united two rival branches of the Medici family: his mother, Maria Salviati, was the granddaughter of Lorenzo the Magnificent. His father was the great-grandson of Lorenzo il Vecchio (Cosimo's brother).

Cosimo I, Grand Duke of Tuscany

Cosimo I (1519-1574) was only 18 when he assumed power in 1537, but he proved an able and politically astute leader. He consolidated his power, conquering Siena and Lucca to become the Grand Duke of Tuscany in 1569.

Politically ruthless, he was also highly cultured. He promoted arts and education and established the Accademia della Crusca, charged with promoting the Tuscan dialect which has become the standard Italian used today.

Cosimo I established the Uffizi as his centre of administration and began a small museum for the Medici art collection. He laid the foundations of the Medici rule which would continue in Tuscany for the next two hundred years.

The End of the Dynasty

In 1737, a dissolute lout, Gian Gastone de Medici, died. He was the last Medici to be Duke of Tuscany. The Duchy passed to the Duke of Lorraine, husband to the Austrian Empress, Maria Therese.Gian's sister, Anna Maria, bequeathed all Medici art and property to the State on the condition that they never leave Florence.

Medici Coat-of-Arms

Originally red balls on a gold shield, but now faded with time, the Medici coat of arms is prominently displayed all over Florence and Tuscany: on buildings and fortifications either financed with Medici money or conquered by Medici armies. One disgruntled subject declared that, *'He has emblazoned even the monks' privies with his balls.'*

The origin is unclear: stories of knights and giants compete with pawnbrokers' emblems and apothecaries' symbols. Whatever the source, in times of danger Medicean supporters were rallied with cries of *Palle! Palle! Palle!*, a reference to the balls *(palle)* on their armour. Originally there were 12; in Cosimo's time it was seven; the ceiling of San Lorenzo's Sagrestia Vecchi has eight; the tomb of Cosimo I has five; and the Ferdinando I coat-of-arms has six.

MEDICI COAT OF ARMS IN SIENA'S CAMPO

San Lorenzo Basilica and Biblioteca

Basilica: 07.30-12.00,15.30–18.30 daily
Mass at 08.00, 09.30, 18.00 Monday-Saturday, 11.00 Sunday and
Holidays
Biblioteca: 09.00–13.00 Monday-Saturday
map D2

Do not be put off by the plain façade of San Lorenzo. This
was the parish church of the Medici family and it houses
a wealth of treasures, including works by Michelangelo
and Donatello as well as the library of Greek and Roman
classics begun by Cosimo il Vecchio.

In 1518, Pope Leo X commissioned Michelangelo to
build the façade. However, the great artist was unable
to make a decision on which of his many designs to
choose. Michelangelo wanted to use marble from Carrara
while the pope wanted to use marble from his quarries
at Pietrasanta. Michelangelo stubbornly held out: a road
had to be specially built to transport the marble from
Carrara to Florence. Then the quarrymen went on strike
over low wages. Two years later the infuriated Pope Leo
cancelled the contract. Michelangelo's façade was never
completed.

In San Lorenzo you can trace the Medici family story.
The early sacristy, commissioned by Cosimo il Vecchio,
is simple and elegant, designed by Brunelleschi and
decorated by Donatello. Michelangelo's tomb for the
murdered Giuliano de Medici (*Tomb For The Duke Of
Nemours*) is a poignant allegory to Night, Day, Dawn and
Dusk. Notice that Dusk is not quite finished.

Cosimo I planned the Medici mausoleum behind the
chancel, but it was his son Ferdinando I who began the
project in 1605.

Witness the ostentatious testament to wealth and power
that is the Chapel of the Princes.

The Dominicans and Savonarola

St Dominic (1170-1221) and St Francis (1181-1226) were friends. Both formed monastic orders: the Franciscan in 1209, the Dominican in 1216. The orders followed a similar theology, but with very differing approaches: Franciscans were against acquiring material wealth and the Dominicans were against heresy. Franciscans wore robes of plain brown sackcloth while the Dominicans dressed in robes of white with a blue cape.

San Marco was the Dominican order to which the powerful preacher Girolamo Savonarola (1452-1498) belonged. Though he was small in stature, his sermons influenced all of Florence to renounce conspicious consumption in favour of a regimented life spent meditating on the cross. The Santa Maria del Fiore (Duomo) was packed when Savonarola spoke. Early on, even Lorenzo Medici was forced to admire his courage in speaking out against the corruption of the popes.

When Lorenzo died, Savonarola correctly predicted the Medici's exile, the coming of the plague and the invasion of Florence by French armies. He stepped into the power vacuum left by the Medici and adopted a democratic constitution with himself at its head in 1494.

Under his tyrannical rule, women were forbidden to enter the church or walk the streets without a chaperone. Gangs of vigilantes roamed the streets searching for homosexuals and prostitutes who were often brutally murdered. Bright colours were no longer allowed to be worn and strict morality laws were enforced for four years until the crop failure of 1498 turned the people against him.

A Franciscan monk challenged a Dominican to a public ordeal to prove Savonarola's teachings to be true or false. The ordeal was cancelled but an angry mob, looking for blood, seized Savonarola. A quick trial found him guilty and he was hung and then burnt in the Piazza Signoria.

Convent of San Marco

09.00-14.00 Tuesday-Sunday.
map E1

In striking contrast to the zealotry of Savonarola is the Dominican monk and painter, Fra Angelico (1400-1455). He was nicknamed *Angelico* because of his reputation for sweetness and humility: it is said he couldn't paint a crucifixion without weeping. His beautiful frescoes are to be found in the Hospice and Cloister of San Marco. The entrance is beside the church.

The paintings were commissioned to inspire the monks to greater faith and his works decorate the simple cells that once were the living quarters of the monks. His most famous and most copied work is the *Annunciation* which is found on the first floor.

Fra Angelico was beatified in 1984 by Pope John Paul II and he is the patron saint of artists.

Savonarola's cells are at the end of the corridor on the first floor.

Santa Maria Novella

Piazza di Santa Maria Novella
map C2
055 210 113
07.00-12.15, 15.00-18.00
Monday-Friday
08.00-1200, Saturday
15.30-17.00 Sunday

A Dominican church
completed in 1357. Worth
visiting for:
Giotto's *Crucifix*
Masaccio's fresco *Trinity*
Ghirlandaio's fresco cycle *The
Life of John the Baptist.*
Brunelleshi's *Crucifix*

(Story p 34)

Santa Maria del Carmine
Brancacci Chapel

Piazza del Carmine
map B4
055 238 2195
10.00-13.00,15.00-17.00
Wednesday-Monday
13.00-17.00 Sunday

Famous for Masaccio's frescoe
cycle *The Life of St Peter.* In the
frescoe, *The Expulsion of Adam
and Eve* portrayed the depth
of human emotion for the first
time. See page 33 for more on
the artist.

San Spirito

Piazza di Santa Spirito
map B4

055 210 030
08.00-1200, 16.00-18.30 daily
08.00-12.00 Wednesday

This Augustinian church
designed by Brunelleschi
dates from 1520.

The interior has the graceful
columns Brunelleschi
loved, but the harmony and
simplicity has been spoilt by
the Baroque high altar.

There are 38 side altars
decorated with paintings by
Ghirlandaio and Lippi.

San Miniato al Monte

Via del Monte alle Croci
map F5
055 234 2731
08.00-19.30 daily in summer
08.00-17.30 in winter

A beautiful Romanesque
jewel-box church located
above the Piazzale
Michelangelo. It was built
over a shrine to St Miniato an
Armenian Christian beheaded
for his beliefs in the 3rd
century. There is a panoramic
view of the hills of Florence
from the church.

Santa Croce
Piazza di Santa Croce
map F4
055 244 619
Basilica open:
8.30-18.30 daily in summer
7.30-12.30, 15.00-18.30 winter
Museo, Cloister, Pazzi Chapel
summer opening:
10.00-12.00, 14.30-18.30 daily
15.00-17.00 in winter

A dark Franciscan church containing the tombs of Michelangelo, Galileo and Machiavelli.

Giotto's frescoes are in the Bardi Chapel (in the basilica), as is Donatello's *Crucifix*. Both require a coin to light the interior.

Brunelleschi designed the domed Pazzi Chapel which was commissioned by the Pazzi family before the Medici assassination plot.

Cimabue's *Crucifixion* and Taddeo Gaddi's *Last Supper* are in the Museo.

The entrance to the leather school is at the side of the church and through the cloister.

(Story p 34)

SANTA CROCE CHURCH

Archivo Alinari

Largo Fratelli Alinari, 15
map C1
055 239 51
09.00-13.00 Monday-Friday

The Alinari brothers were photographers in and around Florence at the height of the Grand Tour (p 68). They photographed the city and its tourists from 1840 and continued until the turn of the century. The archive of quality photographs, prints and postcards gives a fascinating insight into the life of Florentines during the Victorian era.

Palazzo Rucellai

Via della Vigna Nuova, 16
map C2

Giovanni Rucellai made his fortune from importing red dye made from lichen trees found only on Majorca. Red was a sought after colour for garments because it was affordable only to the rich. Wearing red was a sign of conspicious consumption and was forbidden in the time of Savanorola. The Palazzo, by Leon Battista Alberti, was the first in Florence to follow strict rules of classical design.

Giovanni Rucellai's son married Cosimo il Vecchio's granddaughter. The Palazzo's frieze features the family heraldic emblems entwined.

Casa di Dante

Via Santa Margherita, 1
map E3
055 219 416
10.00-18.00 Wed.-Monday
April-January
10.00-16.00 January-March

Although it is uncertain that the poet Dante actually lived here, the house has artifacts from his life and includes the first hand-written translations of the *Divine Comedy*.

Museo di Firenze ComíEra

Via dell'Oriuolo, 24
map E2
055 239 8483
10.00-13.00 daily
closed Thursday

Traces the development of the city of Florence through drawings, plans and paintings.

Museo Archeologico

Via della Colonna, 38
map F1
055 235 75
08.30-14.00 daily

Etruscan bronzes, including the original bronze Chimera (300 BC) from the fountain in Arezzo.

Museo Horne

Via de' Benci, 6
map E4
055 244 661
09.00-13.00 Monday–Saturday

Houses a small collection of paintings and sculpture left to the city by English art historian Herbert Percy Horne. The most important work is Giotto's 13th century altarpiece of Saint Stephen.

Museo di Storia della Scienza

Piazza de Giudici, 1
map D4
055 293 493
09.30-13.00 Monday-Saturday
14.00-17.00 Monday, Wednesday and Friday

A small museum mostly dedicated to the Pisa born scientist and court mathematician to the Medici, Galileo Galilei (1564-1642).

Exhibits include his telescopes used to discover the largest moons of Jupiter.

Outside Florence

Petraia

The Medici Villa

Villa Medicea Della Petraia
Via della Petraia, 40
055 452 691
08.15-20.00 daily in summer
earlier closing in winter
closed 2nd & 3rd Monday each month

Commissioned by Cardinal Ferdinando in 1576. The gardens are particularly worth visiting and include a moat to the front of the building and a park to the rear. The courtyard has frescoes showing the history of the Medici. Take the No 28 bus from Santa Maria Novella bus station.

Caiano

Villa di Poggio a Caiano

Piazza dei Medici, 12
055 877 012
9.30-18.30 daily in summer
09.30-17.30 in winter

Sumptuously decorated and set in magnificent gardens, this villa was also the residence of the Savoys.

The Boboli Gardens

Rear of the Pitti Palace
09.00-19.30 or 1 hour before
sunset in winter.
closed 1st and 4th Monday of
the month.
map C5

Situated behind the Pitti
Palace, these are the largest
gardens in the centre of
Florence. They are laid out
on two main levels: the
lower features 17th century
arboured walks, the higher
garden with fruit trees has a
lovely view over the valley.

Trees are mainly evergreen
with large double hedges and
seasonal flowers. The walks
are lined with numerous
statues: many of them
restored Roman works, others
dating from the 16th and 17th
centuries. At the top is the
secluded Cavalier Garden
with a gallery displaying a
large collection of Viennese
porcelain.

BOBOLI GARDENS

Le Cascine
Lungarno Amerigo Vespucci
at Ponte della Vittoria
off map

Florence's largest park is located to the west of the city centre along the Arno. There is a swimming pool and a place to rent roller blades. Playgrounds are scattered throughout the park which is at its busiest on Sundays.

Canadian Island
Via Gioberti, 15
off map
055 677 567
15.30-18.30 Monday-Friday in summer and also 9.00-13.00 winter Saturdays
closed August

An English-speaking environment where children can play with Italian children learning English.

Piscina Nannini
Lungarno Aldo Moro, 6
off map
055 677 521
10.00-18.30, 20.00-22.30
in summer only

An Olympic-size pool located west of the city centre. The roof slides back to make an open-air pool.

Bonsai Gardens
Borgo Pinti, 74
map F2
09.00-13.00 Sundays
free entrance.

A small garden in the Santa Croce district. Formerly a car park, now a lovely garden with many different types of Bonsai and Suseiki trees. Makes a pleasant outing for a Sunday morning.

Giardino dei Semplici
Via Micheli, 3
map E1
09.00-13.00 Monday-Friday

Located just north-east of the convent of San Marco.

The name means garden of samples.

Designed by Niccolo Tribolo for Cosimo I in 1545. It was founded to research and collect sample varieties of medicinal plants, as well as those used to make perfumes.

Fossils, minerals and rare botanicals are found in the garden, which now also has a collection of tropical plants.

The Grand Tour

As Italians led the way in the Renaissance, the influence of Italian culture increasingly came to dominate Europe during the 16th century. Even Shakespeare felt its influence: *Romeo and Juliet* was adapted from a play written by Luigi da Porto of Vincenza in the 1520s.

The term Grand Tour was first coined in 1670 by Richard Lassels. He wrote what is considered to be the first travel guide written in the English language: *The Voyage of Italy, or A Compleat Journey Through Italy in Two Parts*. His book had a huge impact on a generation of upper class young for whom it would become *de rigueur* to take the Tour in order to completely understand the *'elements and alphabet of breeding'*.

The route was strictly proscribed and was expected to take up to three years: beginning with a lengthy visit to Florence and Tuscany; followed by Rome and Naples, being sure to visit Pompeii and Paestum; and then beginning the journey homewards in time to visit Venice for Ascension Day, in order to see the grand festival of the marriage of Venice with the sea.

Subsequent written accounts made by various 'tourists' proved influential: travel to Italy grew massively in the 18th century. An alpine crossing was used by the majority of travellers in preference to sea travel with its unpredictable storms and the threat of pirates. In 1780, forty thousand Britons were being carried in litters across the Alps to Florence. William Beckford's second Grand Tour was so grand the Italians mistook him for visiting royalty and it was rumoured that William was really the Emperor of Austria.

Travellers usually went in retinues of up to 20 people, including a tutor, who was charged with making the young aristocrat into a man, educating him in all ways. While the Tour was at its height less than a third of British aristocracy attended Oxford and Cambridge, so it was the Tour's function to develop the elite and educate young patricians for future government.

Rome was the fulfillment of a dream for many on the Grand Tour. The Colosseum and the Forum rendered many travellers speechless; it became fashionable to view the ruins by moonlight to lessen the overwhelming assault on the senses. It was also necessary to have one's portrait painted while by posing beside the Colosseum, as proof that the subject had really been on the Grand Tour and seen Rome. This was an essential purchase so that, when he returned home, he could show himself to be a man of taste, versed in the classics and antiquity.

In Naples, the British ambassador to the court, William Hamilton, was renowned as an expert on all things Italian: his treatises were taken as gospel by the Grand Tourists. Ancient artifacts in his possession formed the basis of the collection at the British Museum. His wife, Emma Hamilton, and her tendency to pose in revealing Grecian tunics, was also a strong incentive to extend one's visit.

Conflict in Europe stopped the Grand Tour for a brief time. After the Napoleonic Wars ended in 1815 the Tour resumed, but in a different form. The 19th century saw many visits by the Romantic poets: Byron, Shelley, Keats and Browning composed lengthy poems about the beauty of Italy, its landscape, art and people. These were widely read amongst the aristocracy in Britain.

Later in the century, train travel made it possible for family groups and young ladies with chaperones to make the journey. This was the era of E.M. Forster's *A Room with a View*. American writers such as Henry James and Mark Twain made what was now called the 'European Tour' fashionable for Americans during Victorian times.

Elizabeth Barrett Browning
from 'Aurora Leigh'

I found a house at Florence on the hill
Of Bellosguardo. 'Tis a tower which keeps
A post of double observation o'er
That valley of Arno (holding as a hand
The outspread city) straight toward Fiesole
And Mount Morello and the setting sun,
The Vallombrosan mountains opposite,
Which sunrise fills as full as crystal cups
Turned red to the brim because their wine is red.
No sun could die nor yet be born unseen
By dwellers at my villa: morn and eve
Were magnified before us in the pure
Illimitable space and pause of sky,
Intense as angels' garments blanched with God,
Less blue than radiant. From the outer wall
Of the garden, drops the mystic floating grey
Of olive trees (with interruptions green
From maize and vine), until 'tis caught and torn
Upon the abrupt black line of cypresses
Which signs the way to Florence. Beautiful
The city lies along the ample vale,
Cathedral, tower and palace, piazza and street,
The river trailing like a silver cord
Through all, and curling loosely, both before
And after, over the whole stretch of land
Sown whitely up and down its opposite slopes
With farms and villas.

Robert Browning

from 'Up at a Villa—Down in the City'

Had I but plenty of money, money enough and to spare,
The house for me, no doubt, were a house in the city-square;
Ah, such a life, such a life, as one leads at the window there!
Something to see, by Bacchus, something to hear, at least!
There, the whole day long, one's life is a perfect feast;
While up at a villa one lives, I maintain it, no more than a beast.

Well now, look at our villa! Stuck like the horn of a bull
Just on a mountain-edge as bare as the creature's skull,
Save a mere shag of a bush with hardly a leaf to pull!
I scratch my own, sometimes, to see if the hair's turned wool.

But the city, oh the city – the square with the houses! Why?
They are stone-faced, white as a curd, there's something to take the eye!
Houses in four straight lines, not a single front awry;
You watch who crosses and gossips, who saunters, who hurries by;
Green blinds, as a matter of course, to draw when the sun gets high
And the shops with fanciful signs which are painted properly.

Is it ever hot in the square? There's a fountain to spout and splash!
In the shade it sings and springs; in the shine such foam-bows flash
On the horses with curling fish-tails, that prance and paddle and pash
Round the lady atop in her conch—fifty gazers do not abash,
Though all that she wears is some weeds round her waist in a sort of sash.

But, bless you, it's dear—it's dear! Fowls, wine at double the rate.
They have clapped a new tax upon salt, and what oil pays passing the gate
It's a horror to think of. And so, the villa for me, not the city!
Beggars can scarcely be choosers; but still—ah, the pity, the pity!

Charles Dickens
from Nicholas Nickleby

There was a bubble.
The bubble burst.
Four rich nobleman took villa residences in Florence
Four hundred nobodies were ruined
And one of them was Nicholas Nickleby.

Thomas Hardy
'In the Old Theatre, Fiesole'

I traced the Circus whose gray stones incline
Where Rome and dim Etruria interjoin,
Till came a child who showed an ancient coin
That bore the image of a Constantine.

She lightly passed; nor did she once opine
How, better than all books, she had raised for me
In swift perspective Europe's history
Through the vast years of Caesar's sceptred line.

For in my distant plot of English loam
'Twas but to delve, and straightway there to find
Coins of like impress. As with one half blind
Whom common simples cure, her act flashed home
In that mute moment to my opened mind
The power, the pride, the reach of perished Rome.

The village of Fiesole is an old Etruscan city high in the hills above Florence. It has substantial Roman and Etruscan remains and has been a popular summer retreat since the Middle Ages. Today only footballers and the elite can afford to purchase a villa here, but its hilltop position and fresh breezes make it a lovely place to walk and escape the heat of the city.

The Gucci Family

Guccio Gucci (1881-1953) did not want to go into the family millinery business. His father made straw hats. Guccio wanted to work with leather, not straw. He ran away to London where he worked at the Savoy hotel.

He returned to Florence in 1905 and opened a modest saddlery store. The finely crafted saddles, boots and other equestrian accessories sold well and the business grew. Guccio's sons Aldo, Vasco and Rodolfo entered the family business. The climate was not a happy one: Guccio was a passionate man who enjoyed a good fight; he encouraged competition between his sons.

Aldo enraged his father by opening a rival Gucci store in Rome in 1938. It was he who created the famous 'double G' logo. He convinced Rodolfo to join him. Together they expanded operations into America and overseas. This was against Guccio's wishes but with his death in 1953 his power ceased. Aldo's son Paolo expanded the brand so it appeared on everything from perfumes to glasses to toilet paper.

Guccio Gucci had built a business on the loafer: a conservative and practical slip-on shoe made of soft, Florentine leather; a shoe synonymous with wealth, taste and class. Guccio's sons, Aldo and Rodolfo were now watching his grandsons cheapen the brand. Profits were booming and so were the arguments in the boardroom: Paolo exposed his father's tax evasions which resulted in Aldo's imprisonment. Paolo was sacked: his cousin Maurizio was named president.

Maurizio, Rodolfo's son, had married Patrizia against his father's wishes. They were divorced in 1985. However, Patrizia was unhappy with her divorce settlement of US $1 million. Her rage sent her into therapy. Maurizio was gunned down in front of his office in 1995. Patrizia and her psychiatrist were found guilty in 1998 of hiring Maurizio's killer.

Designer Outlets

Gucci and Prada have wholesale outlets on the outskirts of Florence that offer substantial savings.

Gucci
Via Aretano, 63
055 865 7775
9.30-18.00 Monday-Saturday

Located about 30-40 minutes drive south-east of Florence on the road to Arezzo.

Prada
055 919 0580
9.30-19.00 Monday-Saturday

Located outside the village of Levanella. From Florence take the A1 motorway, exit at Valdarno and follow the signs for Montevarchi.

Flagship Shops

Ferragamo
Via de Tornabuoni, 16r
055 292 123

The family shoe business has expanded to clothing and accessories. A museum dedicated to Salvatore Ferragamo, founder of the business, is on the top floor. Viewing by appointment only.

Gucci
Via de Tornobuoni, 73r
055 264 011

High fashion and accessories at high prices.

Clothing and Accessories

Florentine leather is renowned for its fine detail: a large quantity of coats, jackets, trousers, belts and handbags are available for all tastes. Ready-made clothing in Florence has a special elegance and originality. The local delicate embroidery on lingerie is well known.

Leather School

A leather-crafting school and shop is situated in the cloister behind Santa Croce. Leather bags and coats are made to a high quality on the premises using traditional methods. Prices are expensive but the quality is superior.

San Lorenzo

This part of town is famous for the San Lorenzo street market: one of the best places in Florence to purchase leather goods. Bartering is acceptable. It doesn't always work but is worth a try. Check the seams for quality.

THE LEATHER MARKET

Soap and Perfume

Farmacia Antica is in Via della Scala, the street that goes back towards the station from the church of Santa Maria Novella. They sell hand-made soaps and perfumes made by nuns and monks in various parts of Tuscany using antique recipes. Also visit the Antique Herbalist just off Piazza Signoria: the interior is covered in frescoes and has delicious fragrances, pot pourri, cosmetics and soaps.

Gold and Silver

The Ponte Vecchio is the place to purchase fine silver and gold, precious stones and filigree. Florentine mosaics in semi-precious stones are also to be found here.

Hand-Made Paper and Leather Bound Book

Hand marbled paper is a specialty of Florence. Many shops sell letter paper, note pads and thank-you cards. They are easy to fit into your suitcase and make excellent gifts and note cards when you return home.

Leather bound books of marbled or ragged paper are also specialities. There are some excellent shops to be found on the streets between the Piazza Signoria and the Santa Croce church.

Shoes and Bags

You will most likely be overwhelmed by the variety and quantity of shoe and bag shops. Florence is also a great place to buy your luggage.

Daniel Day Lewis took a hiatus from the film industry to work in a leather goods shop across the river in Oltrarno.

For a more detailed listing of shops see the shopping section towards the back of this book.

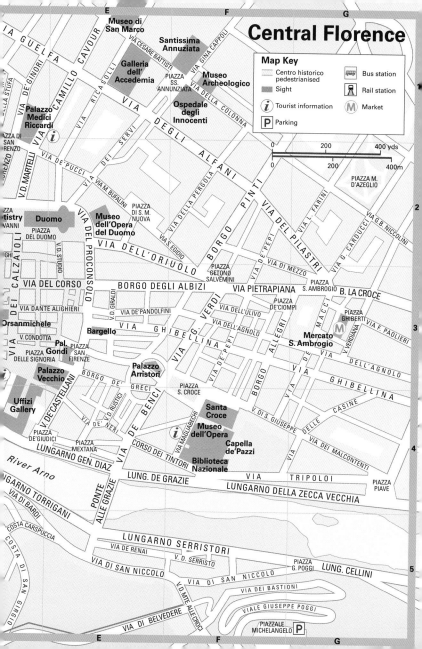

Introducing Siena

This beautiful medieval city is a must for anyone visiting Tuscany. The heart of the city is the unique shell-shaped Piazza del Campo, known locally as *il Campo*. This is a perfect spot to relax and enjoy a gelati at one of the many outdoor cafes. It may be an expensive ice cream but if you consider that you are renting a seat in Siena's exclusive outdoor theatre, the price becomes reasonable.

Sitting along the edge of the sloping Campo you can almost see the knights on horseback and hear the trumpets blare. Twice a year, on 2nd July and on 16th August, the Sienese faithfully recreate their medieval heritage in the *Palio*, a sumptuous pageant-cum-horse race around the Campo.

The Campo contains nine sections, commemorating the beneficent rule of the Council of Nine who governed Siena from the mid-13th to the early 14th century. This was a period of exceptional stability.

'The Nine' made the decision to build the Campo using the local bricks, which have a distinctive reddish-brown colour. *Terra di Siena* is the pigment used to make the paint colours Raw Sienna and Burnt Sienna.

The Sienese have a proud look and dress neatly in the earthy colours of Siena's buildings. They keep their city clean and frown on litter: visitors are encouraged to use the numerous bins around town.

THERE IS A MARKET ON WEDNESDAY MORNING. FINDING A PLACE TO PARK ON THIS DAY MAY BE A CHALLENGE AND SIENA WILL BE BUSIER THAN NORMAL.

Allegories of Good and Bad Government

The Sala dei Nove in the Palazzo Pubblico was the meeting room of the Council of Nine. One of the first landscape paintings of the Renaissance is found here. Ambrogio Lorenzetti's *Allegory of Good and Bad Government* was completed in 1338. The brief was for a painting to decorate the council chamber of the Nine, so that it *'please the eye, bring joy to the heart and satisfy every one's senses; to the glory of the whole community that the leaders and rulers of the commune should enjoy surroundings which are fine, beautiful and honourable.'*

The governing elite were the only people allowed into the chamber to view the painting. Therefore, the picture illustrates the obligations of the governors to the governed. It depicts medieval Siena divided into two halves: *Good Government* and *Bad Government.*

In *Good Government,* Siena is the home of Concord, Justice and Peace, truly a City of God. The dominant figures in *Good Government* represent the virtues needed for the life of the good citizen. Common Good sits in the middle with Peace, Fortitude, and Prudence on his right; Magnanimity, Fortitude and Prudence on his left. Faith, Hope and Charity hover above him.

In the medallions above *Bad Government* are dark planets: Saturn, Jupiter and Mars. Siena's houses are demolished, its countryside devastated, clearly illustrating the consequences of tyranny.

You will also see the coat-of-arms of the Guelph. Siena was the most Ghibelline of all Italian cities, therefore anything Guelph must be considered bad. Their allegiance to the Ghibelline faction continued, even through the 14th century when the Sienese were forced into declaring nominal allegiance to the Guelphs.

The Palio

To a Sienese, the Palio is the most important matter in the world and it is said that: *'We do not play at the Palio. We live it.'*

The Palio occurs twice in each summer, on 2nd July to commemorate the miracles of the Madonna of Provenzano, and on the 16th August to honour the Assumption of the Virgin.

Ten horses are ridden in a bareback race around the Campo for ninety seconds in a fiercely competitive expression of ritualized violence. Each hired jockey wears the colours of his *contrada* and a helmet to protect him from the shower of blows which will be rained upon him by other jockeys. It is forbidden to seize hold of another jockey or horse's reins. Otherwise, the horse race is a no-holds barred event acting out the rivalry of the *contrade*.

Within the context of the Palio there still exists the *vendetta*. Events which occur during the Palio, especially betrayals, are never forgiven or forgotten and revenge is certain to be exacted in the future.

The Palio is the most important act of worship in the Sienese calendar. The preparations of each contrada take place in a religious context: the banner which is the prize – the Palio itself – is decorated with a representation of the Blessed Virgin, and the patron saints of each contrada are intimately concerned with the outcome of the race. Before the race each horse is taken into the contrada church to be blessed. It is considered good luck if the horse defecates during the blessing.

On the morning of the race, mass is said in the Campo to consecrate the event and render the Campo a sacred place. After the event, the winning contrada is obliged to give thanks: in the church of Provenzano in July, in the cathedral in August.

The Contrada

You do not choose your membership into a contrada, you are born into it. Each contrada serves as a social club and church congregation. A member of a contrada who is in need will often be assisted with contrada funds, perhaps without having to request such assistance.

The contrada gives an identity to all citizens of Siena. No man or woman is anonymous within the contrada, each being small enough for all members to be known to the others and their church priests.

Rivalries between the contrada are intense, and often are hereditary, with origins long forgotten. In 1729 each was assigned a specific territory within Siena, creating boundaries which have divided the Sienese against themselves while uniting them against the rest of the world.

Each contrada is a self-governing community with its own general council and officials who are elected annually on the second Sunday in May. The supreme head of the contrada is the Prior, Rector or Governor who is assisted by councillors and other officials. The Captain publicly represents the contrada during the Palio.

Throughout Siena's history, the vitality of the *contrade* has been essential to the civic health of the city. By an act of dedication to his contrada and his city, through the Palio, the Sienese citizen discovers both a personal and corporate identity. Fighting and violence over contrada matters is tolerated during the Palio festival by a society that accepts no other expression of public lawlessness.

Siena's reported crime rate is amongst the lowest in the world.

Contrade

Aquila	Eagle
Bruco	Caterpillar
Drago	Dragon
Giraffa	Giraffe
Istrice	Hedgehog
Leocorno	Unicorn
Lupa	Wolf
Nicchio	Shell
Oca	Goose
Onda	Wave
Pantera	Panther
Selva	Game bird
Tartaruga	Tortoise
Torre	Tower
Chiocciola	Snail
Civetta	Owl
Valdimontone	Ram

Palio Race Events

It can be very expensive to get tickets to the actual Palio as they are sold out for years in advance, however there are many events leading up to the big race.

Three days before

Horses are presented for selection at the town hall and allotted to ten of the 17 contradas which have been selected to run in this Palio.

First trial race in the Piazza del Campo at 19.15

Two days before

Second trial race at 09.00

Historical procession with all contradas bearing their flags at 17.00

Third trial race at 19.15

Outdoor concert in the Piazza at 21.30

One day before

A service in the Duomo to honour Catherine, the patron saint of Siena.

Fourth trial race at 09.00
Prova Generale at 19.15

On the eve of the Palio, each contrada hosts a banquet for all members.

Race day

Final trial race at 09.00

The Blessing of each horse and jockey at the contrada parish church.

Procession through Siena at 16.45

Run of the Palio 19.00

The morning after the race

The winning contrada parades through the streets of Siena towards their parish church for a blessing.

Everyone celebrates with a gigantic meal and party that lasts for several days.

PALIO PARADE

Siena Cathedral

Dedicated to the Assumption and considered to be the earliest of the great Tuscan Gothic churches. The cathedral was begun in 1196; the main structure completed by 1215. Many ordinary citizens helped to cart the black and white stones used in its construction from quarries on the outskirts of the city. Inside, black and white marble pillars support the vault. The inlaid marble floor is stunning.

In 1339, the Sienese decided to build a new nave, with the aim of making it the biggest church in Christendom. The plan came to naught when the plague hit the city in 1348, killing off much of the population. The unfinished nave now forms an archway over the path leading to the town and contains a museum of Gothic sculpture.

Ospedale di Santa Maria della Scala

Opposite the Duomo is Siena's hospital, which was founded in the 9th century by a cobbler name, Sorore. He established a hostel for the many pilgrims passing through Siena on their way to Rome. Sorore's mother had a vision of babies ascending into heaven on a golden ladder and was inspired to add a foundling hospital to the hostel.

The Sienese have always been meticulous about health. They insisted on the washing of hands and sterilization of instruments as early as the 14th century. Iron beds were used to halt the spread of bedbugs; patient's diets were adapted to their illness. To encourage hospital donations the Sienese were permitted to deduct these gifts from their taxes; many left huge sums in their wills.

The plague of 1348 killed 2/3 of the population in one year, some 70,000 citizens. Paradoxically, it generated great wealth for the hospital, which was invested in research and the commissioning of artworks.

Rooms were decorated with beautiful art: it was believed that this would inspire positive thoughts to encourage recuperation.

The hospital is gradually being turned into a museum and no longer accepts overnight patients, but doctors still consult here. The *Meeting of San Joachim and Anne* fresco is in the chapel on the left.

Meeting of San Joachim and Anne   91

Central Siena

Map Key

- Centro historico pedestrianised
- Sight
- *i* Tourist information
- P Parking
- Bus station
- Rail station
- M Market

SAN GIMIGNANO

Medieval Manhattan

San Gimignano is on a hill 324 metres high, overlooking Val d'Elsa. The town is built on the site of an Etruscan settlement along the main road from Rome to the north of Italy. San Gimignano takes its name from the Bishop of Modena, who died in 387. It was a free commune from the 12th century.

The 13 distinctive towers of San Gimignano are a result of the internal strife and mutual hatred of two families: the Ardinghelli, who were Guelphs, and the Salvucci, who were Ghibellines. Each tried to outdo the other by building the tallest tower. At one time there were 72.

On May 8th 1300, Dante Alighieri was here as an ambassador for the Guelph League of Tuscany, which the town had joined. San Gimignano finally submitted to Florence in 1353. Losing its power and the freedom of the commune, the town decayed economically.

This was the birthplace of the poet Folgore and the mystics Pierre Cattini, San Vivaldo, San Bartolo and Santa Fina. Santa Fina is venerated by the people as the patroness of the town. It is said that at her death the angels rang the bells of San Gimignano and masses of violets flowered on all the towers. The violets renew the miracle every year in March.

The wonderfully evocative film *Tea with Mussolini,* filmed in and around Florence, used San Gimignano as a backdrop for some of its scenes.

The town is very busy during the peak season, especially from 10.00 to 16.00. Cars are not permitted inside the walls. There are several car parks on the roads leading up to San Gimignano.

THE CLOSEST CAR PARK TO THE CENTRE IS AT PORTA SAN GIOVANNI ON THE SOUTH SIDE OF SAN GIMIGNANO.

Chapel of Santa Fina

In a small chapel dedicated to San Gimignano's patron saint is a beautiful fresco cycle *Life of Christ* by Domenico Ghirlandaio. These depict the life of Christ with tenderness and simplicity. Not to be missed.

In the Loggia is Ghirlandaio's *Annunciation.*

The Annunciation

The Collegiata

Also called *Il Duomo*, this Romanesque church dates from the 12th century. Inside are many frescoes of interest, including *Last Judgement, Heaven and Hell* by Bartolo, and *Annunciation* by Jacopo della Quercia.

Adjacent to the Collegiata, the Museum of Sacred Art houses sculptures, corals and sacred vestments from the 14th and 15th centuries.

Etruscan Museum

Same entrance as the Sacred Art museum.

Contains a collection of finds from local excavations, including oil and wine amphoras from the 2nd and 3rd centuries BC.

The Palazzo del Popolo

The Palazzo Nuovo del Podesta (1288-1323), is dominated by the Great Tower, the *Torre Grossa,* at 54m high this is San Gimignano's tallest tower.

CLIMB TO THE TOP FOR A REWARDING VIEW, BUT THE WAY DOWN CAN BE CROWDED IN HIGH SEASON.

Within the Palazzo is the beautiful Dante Hall with frescoes by Lippo Memmi (1317).

Festivals
Tourist Office: Piazza del Duomo, I
0577 94000

A special communal committee prepares the *Summer of San Gimignano* every year, consisting of a number of performance and cultural projects. These include music concerts, films and the National painting prize *Raffaele de Grada.*

Gelateria de Piazza
Piazza della Cisterna

Claims to sell the best ice-cream in the world and may be Tony Blair's favourite, judging by the autographed photo and letter, framed and hanging in a place of honour on the wall. Tories be warned!

Shopping

Shopping here is a treat and there are plenty of souvenirs worth the extra room in your luggage.

Be sure to make the climb up through the central piazza and down the other side to check out the shops on Via San Matteo. Here you will find a shop selling salad bowls and forks carved out of local olive wood and authentic Tuscan straw carry bags. The twisty grain of olive wood makes it last through years of washing-up without splitting. The olive bowls are expensive but the forks are a bargain.

San Gimignano is noteworthy for its production of an excellent white wine from the indigenous Vernaccia grape. *Vernaccia di San Gimignano* was the first to be given the DOC recognition in 1966.

The label *Teruzzi & Puthod* is particularly well respected. The vintners are a husband and wife team; Carmen Puthod is a former prima ballerina of La Scala. The local *Colli Senesi Chianti* is very drinkable. Other local white and red wines are readily available in the shops.

Biscotti is another San Gimignano speciality and can be purchased by the piece or in take-home bags. Italians enjoy the smaller almond biscotti dipped in a sweet white wine for dessert. Children prefer to dip them in hot chocolate.

Dried Tuscan mushrooms are also a good buy. Be sure to try the fresh mushrooms served on *bruschetta* in most of the local eateries.

For a more detailed listing of shops, see the shopping section towards the back of this book.

LUCCA

MADONNA OF SAN MICHELE

Passeggiata delle Mura

Lucca is one of the few towns in Italy to have preserved its surrounding walls intact. The massive 16th century red brick walls that enclose Lucca keep out the noise and traffic but they also contribute to an atmosphere that can feel claustrophobic. Fortunately, at the top of the walls is the *Passeggiata delle Mura*, a tree-lined promenade.

The walls are 12 metres high and consist of 11 curtain walls, ten spur bastions and one platform. Many of Italy's great artists and architects, including Brunelleschi and da Vinci, contributed to building Lucca's fortifications.

The promenade along the top of the ramparts dates from the 15th century, but it was Napoleon's sister, Marie Louise de Bourbon, who had the double avenue of trees planted when she made the walk into a public park. To circle Lucca along the promenade takes an hour or so and there are many views of the mountains in the distance. The walk also offers glimpses into the private gardens of the Lucchesi and benches to relax under the trees.

You'll find many delightful strolls in Lucca, and because the town is flat, you won't overtax your leg muscles. The street grid dates from ancient Rome, making this one of the most easily walkable cities in Tuscany. Bicycles have taken the place of scooters so there is a tranquil atmosphere. American Jazz musician Chet Baker languished in the Lucca prison on drug charges in the 1960s. His Ferrari was parked outside the prison during his incarceration where is sat, covered in dust on the street, unharmed until his release.

Never conquered by the Medici, Lucca was proudly independent until its invasion by Napoleon at the end of the 18th century. The pious Lucchesi once required 70 churches to minister to their spiritual needs. The decorative marble of Lucca's cathedrals give the town its beauty. Keep your eye out for the small frescoes that adorn some of Lucca's buildings.

The Guinigi

The Guinigi family fought for generations to keep Lucca independent of Florence and the Medici.

Torre del Guinigi
Via San Andrea 42
0583 485 24
09.00-21.30 daily March-Sept
10.00-18.00 October
10.00-16.30 November-February
map E3

The Casa Guinigi is distinguished by a 145-foot tower complete with a roof garden planted with holm oaks. Over the centuries the trees' roots have spread down to the room below. Climb to the top for views over Lucca.

Museo Nazionale di Villa Guinigi
Via della Quarquonia
09.30-20.00
0583 583 150
map F3

The palatial family villa is now the home of Lucca's museum and art gallery, hosting exhibitions of Lucchese artists.

TORRE DEL GUINIGI

Duomo di San Martino
Piazza San Martino
0583 957 068
closed 15.30-18.30
map D4

The origins of the cathedral date back to the 11th century. The asymmetrical facade is richly decorated in the Pisan style, with tiers and arcades made from Carrara marble.

The cathedral houses the *Volto Santo* (holy image), a medieval wooden crucifix. Legend says that the crucifix was sculpted by Nicodemus in Palestine and bears an accurate representation of the face of Jesus. It is held in veneration and believed to have miraculous powers. Each year the relic is paraded through Lucca's streets on the 13th September, in celebration of the saint's day.

The cathedral also contains works by Tintoretto, Ghirlandaio, Giambologna and Jacopo della Quercia.

Church of San Michele In Foro
Piazza San Michele
07.30-12.30, 15.00-18.00 daily
map C3

The white marble church in the Piazza San Michele, also dates from the 11th century.

The Pisan-Romanesque facade, with tiers of twisted and carved columns, is topped by a statue of the Archangel Michael slaying a dragon (it was Michael who cast Lucifer out of heaven).

The church contains a lovely terracotta Madonna and Child ascribed to della Robbia and several paintings by Filippino Lippi.

The Madonna on the outside corner of the church is a copy of the original inside by Matteo Civitali.

IN LUCCA, PLACES OF WORSHIP ARE OFTEN CLOSED TO TOURISTS DURING RELIGIOUS SERVICES.

Palazzo dei Guinigi
Via Vittorio Veneto
map 4C

Situated next to the Piazza Napoleone, Lucca's main square is dominated by the Palazzo Guinigi: a stately palace and former residence of the Guinigi family that is now used as the Provincial headquarters.

Cafes and gelati shops are found around the tree-lined piazza. This is a shady place to take shelter from the sun.

Palazzo Pfanner
Via degli Angeli, 33
small entrance fee
map C2

The Palazzo was used as a location for *The Portrait of a Lady*, a film starring Nicole Kidman. It featured as the home of Gilbert Osmond, played by John Malkovitch. The palazzo was purchased by the Controni family from Signore Moriconi, who went broke building the house and fled to Poland. The gardens were added by the Contronis. The crumbling oval-shaped relief, seen at the entrance to the garden, is a sarcophagus from the 3rd century, probably Etruscan. The garden itself is slightly neglected but is peaceful and away from the crowds.

Shopping

Lucca provides excellent shopping with most of the major chains represented. Several shops sell hand-made lace and locally made ceramics. The main shopping street, with many elegant shops, is Via Fillungo.

A CERAMIC WINE STOPPER MAKES AN INEXPENSIVE MEMENTO. THESE ARE ALSO AVAILABLE WITH A MATCHING DISH FOR THE WINE BOTTLE.

In Lucca

Giardino Botanico
Via del Giardino Botanico, 14
09.00-13.00, 15.30-18.30, Tuesday–Saturday
09.00-13.00 Sundays
closed Mondays
entrance fee
map F4

Lucca's gardens, tucked into an angle of the city walls, date from 1820 and include a wide range of native Tuscan plants from alpine to coastal varieties.

Around Lucca

The sub-climate around Lucca is cooler and the ground more fertile, which means that Tuscany's best gardens are to be found near here. Pescia is the centre for Italy's growing flower cultivation industry and hosts a large trade fair every year.

Many villas with beautiful Italianate gardens are in the Pizzorne plateau and are easily accessible from the stretch of motorway between Lucca and Pescia. Recall the age of the *ars topiaria*, the art of the decorative garden in the Renaissance, by visiting the following four gardens:

Villa Garzoni
Piazza della Vittoria, 1
Collodi
0572 429 590
09.00-19.30 daily
entrance fee

These attractive gardens were begun in 1633 and finished around 1800. Designed by Marquis Romano di Alessandro Garzoni, the gardens are based on a Renaissance plan with baroque elements added in the sculpted hedges and fountains. The garden's perspective and symmetry is effective, though ragged at the edges.

Villa Mansi

Segromigno Monte
09.00-13.00, 15.00-18.00

An Italian garden influenced by the formal English country gardens that pre-date Capability Brown. Rooms in the villa are available for rent for special occasions.

Villa Pecci-Blunt

Marlia (formerly known as the Villa Reale)
0583 301 08
11.00-18.00 Tuesday-Sunday, March-November
guided tour hourly

Villa Reale is said to be the best of Lucca's gardens. A jewel that is well worth a visit, the outdoor theatre was the venue for the first Italian production of '*Phaedra*' and is accessed through a wrought-iron gate. The theatre's foyer and stage are delineated by hedges and the stage backdrop is made up of five metre high yew trees. Even the orchestra's raised podium and lighting hoods are fashioned out of hedges.

Villa Torrigiani

Camigliano
0583 928 008
10.00-12.00, 15.00-18.00 Wednesday-Sunday, March-Nov.

This garden was built for the Buonivisi family and features the Luccan tradition of the boulevard -- a double row of cypress trees leading to a villa adorned with statuary. Louis XV's architect, Le Notre is said to have designed the garden to be full of surprises; hidden grottos, fish ponds and brightly coloured flowers. In the 18th century, the garden was partially re-landscaped in the English country style popular at the time.

Puccini

Giacomo Puccini was born in Lucca on December 22 1858, into a family of church musicians. He first studied with his uncle at the Instituto Pacini in Lucca, but a performance of Verdi's *Aida* brought forth a love for operatic composition.

He attended the Milan Conservatory and studied under Bazzini and Ponchielli. His first opera Le Villi was written in 1884, at the age of 26.

Puccini came to live in Torre del Lago, near Viareggio, in 1891. He rented houses until his villa was ready in 1899. The Maestro composed his most successful operas in Torre del Lago: *La Boheme, Tosca* and *Madame Butterfly*. He collaborated with the librettists Illica and Giacosa until the successful team broke up with Giacosa's death in 1906.

Puccini died in Brussels on 29th November, 1924 at the age of 65, before finishing his final opera *Turandot*. The last act was written by Franco Alfano. The great conductor, Leopold Stokowski, later refused to conduct the final act. He told the audience, '*and here the composer laid down his pen,*' and walked off the stage.

Casa Natale di Giacomo Puccini (Puccini's Birthplace)
Corte San Lorenzo, 9 (off Via di Poggio) in Lucca
058 358 4028
10.00-13.00, 15.00-18.00 daily June-September
closed January and February, Mondays in spring and autumn
entrance fee

The house in which Puccini was born is now a museum featuring portraits of the composer and costume designs for his operas.

Torre del Lago

Puccini Opera Festival
Torre del Lago (one hour's drive from Lucca)
058 435 9322
July and August

For a wonderful operatic experience visit the Torre del Lago Festival. It celebrates Puccini's best works and takes place each summer. The stage is built out over the water; the audience sits on the lakeshore.
BRING INSECT REPELLENT

Museo Villa Puccini
Torre del Lago
058 434 1445
10.00-12.30, 15.00-18.30 in summer
14.30-17.00 in winter
closed Mondays and in November.
entrance by guided tour only

Visit the study containing Puccini's piano and portraits of the composer in various periods of his life, as well as the funeral mask from Brussels.

TORRE DEL LAGO

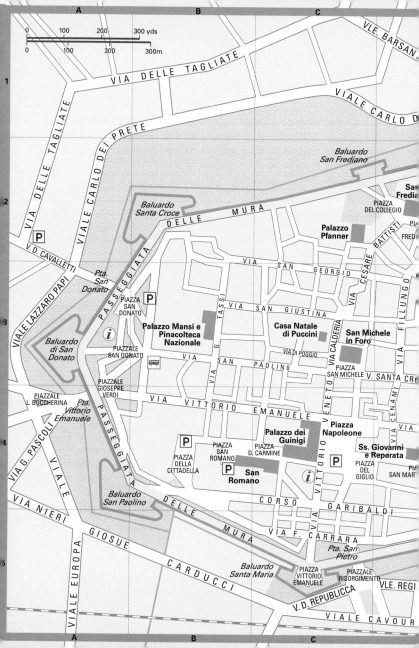

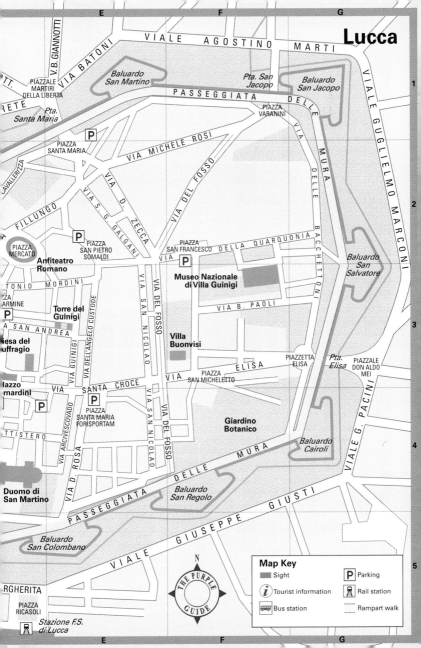

TUSCAN TOWNS

A CORTONA VIEW

Leonardo da Vinci (1452-1519)

He was born on April 15th in Anchiano, the son of playboy attorney Ser Piero da Vinci. Ser was an honorific accorded to respected members of the law guild; Piero was one of three generations of Vinci lawyers. Ser Piero's father, Antonio, was content in the role of country squire and settled on the family lands in Vinci. It was on a visit home that Leonardo was sired with a peasant wench named Catarina, who was soon married off to a man in another village. As a child, Leonardo knew who his mother was, but had very little contact with her. His grandfather Antonio and uncle Francesco raised him. They taught him to read and write, but he was never to receive a complete formal education. Ser Piero continued to live it up in Florence, marrying four times and siring 14 more children.

Leonardo was born a bastard at a time when it was perfectly acceptable to be illegitimate as a royal or a peasant, but to be born illegitimate into the middle-class bourgeoisie was to be ostracised and denied a profession. By disgrace of his birth, Leonardo was barred from a university education and no professional guild would accept him as a member. Ser Piero had just gained the position of notary to the Signoria of Florence when Antonio and Francesco died within days of each other. In his only fatherly act, Piero used his connections to have Leonardo accepted as apprentice to the workshop of Andrea dell Verrochio.

A mediocre artist but an inspiring teacher, Verrochio had studied under Donatello. His workshop was considered the best in Florence. Botticelli was Verrochio's assistant when Leonardo joined in 1469. The workshop was a gathering place of writers, musicians, and famous artists who had once been apprentices, scientists and mathematicians. The young country bumpkin from Vinci soon gained in confidence. Contemporary writers often make reference to Leonardo's physical beauty and note that he began to dress flamboyantly '*favouring rose-coloured tunics reaching only to the knee*'.

Verrochio was a homosexual who lived with his young apprentices, sharing the same rooms and beds. Leonardo was to retain a fondness for beautiful young boys for the rest of his life. At 23, he was arrested for sodomy, a practise that was generally tolerated during the Renaissance. The penalty of the law however, was death by burning at the stake. After four agonising months of retrials and postponements, the case against Leonardo was dismissed.

Leonardo became a Master of the Guild of St Luke and set himself up as an independent artist in 1478. He was to endure three years of being ignored before securing his first commission, from the friars of San Donato at Scopeto, for no fee. However, the friars weren't comfortable with Leonardo's ideas for the *Adoration of the Magi* and arguments were long and numerous. The painting was never completed: Leonardo packed his bags and moved to Milan in the company of a young musician, Atalante Migliorotti.

Between 1482 and 1499 Leonardo was in the service of the Duke of Milan as a painter and engineer. During this time he completed six paintings, including his masterpiece *The Last Supper* (1495-97). He was also a respected hydraulic and mechanical engineer who advised the Duke on architecture, fortifications and military matters.

In 1499 the French armies entered Milan and the Duke was defeated. Leonardo travelled to Mantua, Venice and Urbino where Cesare Borgia employed him as a senior military architect and general engineer. He fled after six months of witnessing Cesare's atrocities, but not before he had befriended Niccolo Machiavelli.

Machiavelli used his influence with the Signori in Florence to secure a commission for Leonardo to paint the *Battle of Anghiari* in the Palazzo Vecchio.

Leonardo began the commission only to find another artist, Michelangelo, painting the *Battle of Cascina* on the opposite wall. They hated each other on first meeting. The locals would soon take great pleasure in visiting the council chamber to catch the latest exchange of insults. Their rivalry came to be known as the '*Battle of the Battles*'. Neither painting was ever finished as both artists were summoned elsewhere: Michelangelo to Rome, to paint the ceiling of the Sistine Chapel; Leonardo to a court in Milan, to answer charges relating to the *Virgin of the Rocks*, which had been rejected by the monks who commissioned the work.

In 1513, Leonardo moved to Rome where he led a lonely life more devoted to mathematical studies and technical experiments in his studio than to painting. After three years of unhappiness Leonardo accepted an invitation from the French king, Francis I.

In France he was known as *first painter, architect, and mechanic of the King*, who allowed him to do as he pleased. The king purchased the *Mona Lisa*, a painting believed to have been started in Florence in 1503. It stayed with Leonardo until its sale.

Leonardo spent his last days arranging and editing his scientific studies. Buried in Saint Florentin, Amboise; his remains were lost when the church was vandalised by Napoleon's army.

He is recognised as a true genius and polymath: a painter, architect, engineer, mathematician, scientist and visionary. Leonardo's ideas for the submarine and the helicopter preceded their invention by several centuries. His paintings are valued as some of the most important works of art that have ever been created.

Piero della Francesca

Piero 1416-1492 was born in Sanselpocro to a family of wool merchants. He was well educated in mathematics and accounting and expected to enter the wool trade. But, Piero convinced his father of his artistic vocation and gained an apprenticeship with the respected painter Antonio di Anghiari.

Florence was at the height of the Renaissance when Piero arrived, and he soon met and was inspired by the great artists working in the city: Brunelleschi, Donatello and especially Masaccio. Competition for commissions was fierce and so Piero left Florence in search of work. He drifted towards home but luckily stopped in Arezzo.

Bicci di Lorenzo was completing a cycle of frescoes based on the *Legend of the True Cross,* for the Chiesa di San Francesco in Arezzo, when he suddenly dropped dead. Another artist had to be found quickly to finish the work. Piero sought the commission but did not have the proof of experience. After long negotiations and the intervention of a powerful family friend, it was decided that Piero could be trusted to complete the fresco cycle.

In 1459, Piero was commissioned by Pope Pius II to paint frescoes for the pontiff's private rooms at the Vatican. Unfortunately, a fire destroyed the works soon after completion. Piero returned to Sanselpocro and painted *The Resurrection* in 1467-1468.

Piero began to slowly lose his sight and increasingly turned towards his childhood studies of mathematics to keep his interest and intellect stimulated. He wrote books on mathematical perspective and geometry in painting, which influenced Leonardo da Vinci.

Piero died on the day Christopher Columbus landed in America, 12th October, 1492.

Arezzo

A capital city rich in culture and beauty is now very popular due to the recent restoration of the frescoes *The Legend of the True Cross*. But don't rush in and out of Arezzo on the *Piero Francesca Trail*, take the time to walk along the colonnade of the Piazza Grande or perhaps join the *passeggiata*: stroll along the Corso Italia, the main street of the centro storico.

The provincial capital of Tuscany, Arezzo was an important town during the Etruscan period. The bronze Chimera in the fountain is a copy of one commissioned in 380 BC, the oldest known casting of bronze. The original resides in the Museo Archeologico in Florence. Arezzo is the birthplace of Petrarch and Michelangelo.

Fiera Antiquaria

On the first Sunday of the month (occasionally Saturday), one of the most important antique fairs in Italy spreads itself along the Corso and down the medieval streets. Items for sale range from furniture and hardware to paintings, books and silver. The Fiera is worth a visit just to see the vendors stretched out on their antique tables having a lunchtime siesta.

Basilica di San Francesco
The Legend of the True Cross
Via Cavour, Piazza San Francesco
0575 900 404
09.00-18.00 Monday-Friday
09.00-17.30 Saturday
13.00-17.30 Sunday
advance booking required: telephone or reserve online

Jacobus da Voragine wrote *The Golden Legend* in the 13th century telling the story of the Holy Wood which was used for the Cross. The story begins with the death of Adam, out of whose mouth the Wood grows. The paintings follow the Holy Wood through time to the triumphant re-entry into Jerusalem, but oddly, never touch on Jesus, or the crucifixion.

Sanselpocro

A pleasant and genteel location, Sanselpocro is pleasant day out and has good restaurants and scenic walks.

Museo Civico
The Resurrection
Madonna of the Mericordia
Palazzo Comunale
Via Aggiunti 65
Piero della Francesca's best loved paintings are in this humble museum.

The Best Picture

Aldous Huxley (1894-1963) claimed to have travelled seven hours by bus from Urbino to view Piero della Francesca's *Resurrection* in Sansepolcro. He obviously thought the long journey worthwhile, later writing an essay arguing that the fresco is *the best picture in the world*.

The fresco had been covered by a thick layer of plaster for two centuries. The plaster protected the paint from damp, preserving the delicate colours which the author describes in loving detail; *subtly sober colours shine out from the wall with scarcely impaired freshness.*

The essay postulates that Piero della Francesca's talent far surpasses better known artists like Botticelli. Huxley even offers to sacrifice (should the need arise) all of Botticelli's works to save Piero's *Resurrection*. His prose on the experience of viewing the extraordinary fresco has inspired many make the journey to Sansepolcro:

> *We need no imagination to help us figure forth its beauty; it stands there before us in entire and actual splendour, the greatest picture in the world.*

And thus began the popular summer pilgrimage known as *The Piero della Francesca Trail,* to see the master's works in Arezzo, Monterchi, Urbino and Sanselpocro.

Castellina in Chianti

Castellina is built around a splendid castle which survives in the centre of the town. It was restored to its pristine condition in 1927. The town also retains its medieval defences, strengthened under Medici rule.

Radda in Chianti

A place for soaking up the slow pace of life and one of the prettiest villages in the Chianti region. Sample local wine accompanied by Tuscan snacks in the local bar. Medieval streets surround the central piazza with its stately Palazzo del Podesta.

Gaiolo in Chianti

This village has a stream running along its main street. The road to the right of the church leads to Spaltenna and on to Vertine, a tiny walled village.

Greve in Chianti

A pretty market town with an attractive colonnaded triangular piazza. The piazza is lined with a number of small shops, mostly selling local wines. There is also a famous butcher known for selling quality wild boar salami and locally made pecorino cheese. (see shopping section p 207)

Certaldo

The town consists of two levels: basso (lower) and alto (higher), the higher being the more historic. Certaldo's narrow streets are lined with restored medieval houses and palazzos. Casa del Boccaccio (now a museum) is where the famous Italian writer is said to have spent his last years.

Monteriggioni

It was mentioned in Dante's `Inferno` and the fortress of Monteriggioni is indeed impressive. Inside the walls in the main square are two excellent restaurants.

Colle di Val D'Elsa

This is a centre of crystal production and sales. A host of outlets sell crystal at very reasonable prices (p 206). The medieval part of Colle is its main attraction and is very photogenic and not too full of visitors. Colle Alto (the upper part) provides a relaxing stop on your journey to Siena.

Volterra

An old Etruscan stronghold with stunning views. Parts of the original walls still exist and the Museo Guarnacci contains the *Ombre della Sera*, an priceless Etruscan antique that was used as a fire-poker by the farmer who unearthed it. The elongated bronze nude figure inspired Giacometti and other modern artists.

The Piazza dei Priori is bordered by medieval buildings, including the Palazzo: a medieval seat of government dating from the 13th century and containing frescoes from the 14th century.

Vinci

Museo Leonardiano di Vinci
Castello dei Conti Guidi
0571 560 55
09:30-18:00 daily
Located in the medieval Castello Guidi, the Leonardo Museum is the main attraction in Vinci.

Inaugurated 15 April, 1953, on the celebration of the fifth centennial of Leonardo's birth, the museum's exhibits are dedicated to Leonardo the inventor and engineer rather than Leonardo the painter.

The displays are large and imaginative: several of Leonardo's drawings have been constructed according to the plans in his notebooks. Displays include what may be considered the first airplane and the precursor to the bicycle, along with water cannon, tanks and unusual gear mechanisms.

Montepulciano

Montepulciano is noted for its red wine, first described as a 'perfect wine' in 1549 by the papal wine steward Sante Lancerio. The wider world did not fully appreciate the finer attributes of *Vino Nobile di Montepulciano* until the 1990s. The past decade has seen the introduction of new *Vino Nobile* producers and an increase in the cultivation of the grape *Prugnolo Gentile*. (vineyards p 201)

The Piazza Grande is the highest point of the town and a popular venue for summer open-air concerts held every year, from the last Saturday in July until mid-August. The Barrels Race, held on the last Sunday of August, is a competition amongst the men of the town who push a 10cwt. barrel up the hills of Montepulciano. The winner of the race is the first to reach the town square. The locals dress in 14th century costumes and there is much pageantry and a procession through the town.

St Agnes is the patron saint of the town and the Church of San Agnese contains her remains. The cathedral dominates the central square and contains '*The Assumption of the Virgin*' by Bartolo.

Montalcino

Montalcino is famous for *Brunello di Montalcino*, one of the world's most distinguished red wines. Other wines produced locally include the *Rossi di Montalcino* and *Moscadello,* a sparkling white wine.

Brunello di Montalcino is the work of Ferruccio Biondi-Santi whose efforts in the vineyards and then in cellars resulted in this fine wine in 1888. Making wine was the family business and Ferruccio's grandfather, Clemente Santi, had won a prize at an agricultural fair in Montepulciano in 1865 with a 'choice red wine, Brunello'.

Brunello di Montalcino only produced three vintages in the first fifty-seven years in 1888, 1891 and 1925 but these were of outstanding quality and fetched a high price. A reputation for exceptional quality and prestige is still attached to Brunello.

The Moscadello grape has a distinguished past; it was served at the English Court of the seventeenth century. (vineyards p 202)

Cosimo 1 provided the town with protection and the Medici arms can be seen from the road that climbs steeply into Montalcino. The Fortress

is open daily and there are fine rooms on the upper floors. Inside the fortress courtyard is a small garden and, on the ground floor, it is possible to taste and buy local wines. Steps lead up to the towers and ramparts and there is a pleasant walk around the medieval walls.

In Sant'Agostino cloister is the *Museo Del Arte Sacra* featuring a collection of Sienese painting and sculpture, including a unique group of wooden life-size figures.

Pienza

Enea Silivo Piccolomini became Pope Pius II in 1458 and set about transforming the insignificant village of his birth into a model town, laid out on clear planning principles. Work advanced so quickly that in three years Pius II was able to elevate the town to an Episcopal See renamed Pienza (after his papal name). After his death the development of the town came to a halt.

Pienza is famous for cheese and honey.

Cortona

Cascading down the southern spur of Monte Egidio, the town commands a magnificent view across to Umbria and Lake Trasimeno. This is one of the loveliest towns in Tuscany and makes an excellent day out.

A very nice lunch can be had in the Osteria del Teatro. Walking the steep slopes will ensure enough exercise to indulge in a sublime Dolci.

Straddling the border between Tuscany and Umbria, Cortona became an official commune in 1200. It was soon caught up in the wars between the Guelph and Ghibelline. The town's position on the hilltop at the junction between two valleys gave it an advantage when fighting off the aggression from both Perugia and Arezzo.

Francesco dei Medici was governor of Cortona in 1570. The Medici balls can be seen amongst the coats-of-arms of Cortona's ruling families in the courtyard of Palazzo Casali, located on Via Casali in the Piazza Signorelli.

Cortona escaped the terrible bombings of World War II. This is attributed to the protection of Santa Margherita. A sculpture in her honour is in Piazza del Duomo.

The Stations of the Cross by Gino Severini on the Via Santa Margherita was completed in 1947 in gratitude for being saved from bombing.

Frances Mayes immortalised Cortona in her bestselling books: *Under the Tuscan Sun* and *Bella Tuscany*. However, fame has its price: Frances tells the story of the American who walked into Bramasole with a video camera and started filming while she and Ed where having a nap! The book has now been made into a film starring Diane Lane.

PARK OUTSIDE THE WALLS AND WALK UP TO THE PIAZZA.

Piazza della Repubblica and Palazzo Passerini

The piazzetta overhanging the Piazza has a beautiful view. The Palazzo was the medieval seat of government and Pope Leo X was a guest here.

Museo Diocesano
The museum is housed in the 16th century Church of the Gesu which is really two separate churches. The lower church was built by Berettini and is accessed by going down a stairway. The upper church has a fresco by Fra Angelico.

Antiques Fair
A popular antiques fair is held during September in the Palazzo Vagnotti.

Summer Centre for Mathematics
The International Summer Centre for Mathematics, together with the University of Pisa, organises conferences and seminars attended by Nobel laureates and other experts in the field.

PIAZZA DELLA REPUBBLICA

Lake Trasimeno

From Cortona it is an easy downhill drive to Lake Trasimeno and a beautiful afternoon promenade.

There are boat trips in the summer, departing from the pier in Passignano. The boat travels across the lake or to visit the islands Isola Maggiore and Isola Polvese.

Castiglione del Lago is an ancient castle situated on a promontory over the lake. The castle is well preserved and can be visited. It is connected to the mainland via a covered walkway to the town hall. Every two years a Kite festival, *Let's Colour the Skies* is held here.

Toro, San Feliciano and Monte Del Lago are some of the other smaller lakeside towns worth a visit.

An Etruscan legend states:

'This lake takes its name from Prince Trasimeno, son of the God Tirreno. The prince met the nymph Agilla, who lived on an island on the lake, fell in love with her and eventually died for her. When a light wind caresses the trees and the water of Lake Trasimeno, a melancholy lament is heard, which is said to be the cry of Agilla searching for the prince. '

LAKE TRASIMENO

Passignano

Set on the northern shores of Lake Trasimeno, Passignano is the liveliest of the lakeside towns and a popular bathing resort.

Passignano is a town in two parts: the medieval section lies on the slopes of a small ridge facing the water, while the more modern town stretches west along the shores of the lake. The local economy relies mostly on tourism, although the ancient fishing industry is also thriving. You will see men and boys fishing off the pier.

Castel Rigone overlooks Passignano and was founded in 543 by Rigone, one of the lieutenants of Totila, king of the Goths. Passignano was an Etruscan and Roman centre for trade as well as a Byzantine stronghold during the Gothic War.

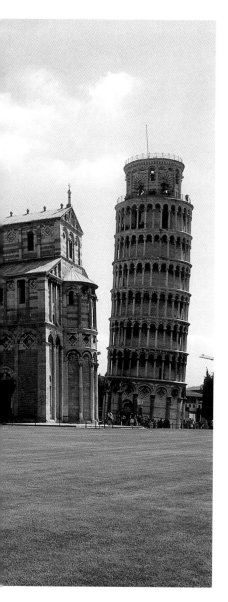

PISA

Introducing Pisa

This is one of Italy's oldest cities: founded by the Greeks, taken over by the Etruscans and conquered by the Romans. The Emperor Hadrian liked to spend his summers here. Later, Arab pirates and Saracens sailed along the coast, plundering towns and carrying away female hostages to sell into slavery.

All Mediterranean seaport towns faced the same threats during the Middle Ages. Pisa built strong defences and developed a maritime empire, which included Sardinia, Corsica and parts of the Balearics. The towns entered into a war with the two other maritime powers: Genoa and Venice. The Pisans lost to Genoa in 1284 and, in the 16th century, Pisa was incorporated into the Medici Duchy of Tuscany. When the river Arno silted up, Pisa lost its access to the sea and thus its power.

Archaeologists recently discovered the remains of ancient Roman ships near the famous Leaning Tower. Because the ships were found so close to the tower, it suggests that the port was situated that far up river. Therefore, the tower was built on an area that was once underwater. Without a proper concrete foundation, the tower leaned. Attempts were made to straighten it later, but even after 11 years of recent work, it still leans!

Pisa today is essentially a university town: one is the state *Universita di Pisa* and the other is private. This means there are many young people riding around on bikes and spending the evenings eating ice cream or having a drink on the *Lungarno* (banks of the Arno). It also means that Pisa has many lively bars and restaurants.

The main artery between the Campo dei Miracoli and the Arno is the Via Santa Maria which is lined with elegant palaces. Look behind the facades at the secret gardens and courtyards; some are open to the public.

Pisa University

First established in the 11th century as a school of law, medicine was added 200 years later. In 1338 Pope Benedict XII placed Bologna University under interdict and closed the institution. The professors moved to Pisa and brought a large following of students.

Pisa sided with the Ghibellines against Florence and the Guelphs. When the Guelphs won, Pisa was closed in favour of Florence. Lorenzo de Medici later closed the university in Florence and moved it back to Pisa.

In 1543, Cosimo I undertook to restore the university, which had fallen on hard times. He convinced Pope Paul III to make large donations from the revenues of the Church. Several new colleges were founded and the university began its specialisation in mathematics and science. Cosimo's friend Galileo taught mathematics and astronomy.

In 1851, the Universities of Pisa and Siena were united; the faculties of law and theology were located at Siena and those of philosophy and medicine at Pisa.

Today the University of Pisa is the rich repository of a millennium of scientific thought. It is recognised throughout Europe for the study of mathematics. Pisa also has schools of engineering, agriculture, veterinary medicine, and pharmacy.

Orto Botanico

Off the Via Santa Maria. Turn right at the Via L. Ghini
08.00-13.00, 14.00-17.30 Monday-Friday
08.00-13.00 Saturday
map D2
The botanical gardens were created by Cosimo I for the university. The institute in the gardens has a facade entirely covered with shells and mother-of-pearl.

Galileo Galilei

Galileo was born in Pisa in 1564, the son of musician Vincenzo Galilei. Vincenzo, who described himself as a nobleman of Florence, carried out experiments on strings to support his musical theories.

Galileo studied medicine at the University of Pisa, but his real interests were always mathematics and natural philosophy. He is chiefly remembered for his work on the velocity of falling objects, his use of the telescope, and his methods of experimentation.

Galileo was Chair of Mathematics at the University of Padua when he caused a stir by discussing more unconventional forms of astronomy and natural philosophy in a public lecture he gave in connection with the appearance of a new star, now called *Keppler's Supernova,* in 1604.

His studies in astronomy were furthered when he learned about a spyglass a Dutchman had demonstrated in Venice. From these reports, and using his own technical skills as a mathematician and craftsman, Galileo made a series of telescopes which improved on the Dutch version.

In 1610, *Message From The Stars* was published in Venice and caused a sensation. The book detailed his astronomical discoveries: Galileo claimed to have seen mountains on the Moon, to have proved the Milky Way was made up of tiny stars, and to have seen four small bodies orbiting Jupiter. These last, he promptly named the *Medicean stars,* hoping to gain favour in Florence.

Galileo had tutored Ferdinand's eldest son, Cosimo II, in mathematics. When Cosimo ascended to the throne in 1610 he nominated Galileo as First Mathematician of the University of Pisa. Galileo was also honoured to be named Mathematician to the Grand Duke of Tuscany.

In Florence Galileo continued his work on motion and mechanics. He became involved in disputes concerning the Copernican theory that all planets, including Earth, revolved around the sun. In 1613 he discovered that, when seen in a telescope, the planet Venus showed phases like those of the Moon, and therefore must orbit the Sun and not the Earth. Most astronomers of the time favoured the Tychonic system in which all the planets except the Earth and Moon orbit the Sun, which in turn goes round the Earth.

With great verbal and mathematical skill, Galileo used his discoveries to support the Copernican system. He made enemies by making his opponents appear foolish. And an Italian made to look foolish will exact his revenge.

It was at the time of the Inquisition that Galileo began to encounter serious opposition to his theory of the motion of the earth. Father Tammaso denounced the opinions of Galileo from the pulpit of Santa Maria Novella, judging them to be erroneous. Galileo was told that he could not defend Copernican astronomy because it went against the doctrine of the Church.

In 1622 he wrote the *The Assayer*, which was approved and published in 1623. Seven years later he returned to Rome to obtain the right to publish his *Dialogue On The Two Chief World Systems,* which was eventually published in Florence in 1632.

In 1633 Galileo was summoned by the Pope to Rome. A tribunal compelled him to renounce his theory, under pain of death. He was forced to deny that the earth and planets moved around the sun. However, he was heard to mumble, *'the Earth does move'*, under his breath.

Andrea Pisano

Andrea Pisano (1290-1348) carved the relief panels on the bronze south door of the Baptistry, and completed Giotto's Campanile, both at the Duomo in Florence.

He was a mere apprentice when he sculpted *Christ and the Apostles* for the St Maria della Spina in Pisa. He also contributed his considerable talent to St Mark's and the Doge's Palace in Venice before working in Florence.

Pisano was Giotto's successor as Master of the Works of the Florence Cathedral. He carved the stone reliefs for the lower register of the Campanile and completed the Orvieto Cathedral which was designed and begun by Lorenzo Maitani.

His two sons, Nino and Tommaso, were also sculptors. The extended Pisano family dominated sculpture and architecture in Pisa for 200 years.

The Leaning Tower

Campo dei Miracoli
map D1
Duomo open: 07.45-12.45, 15.00-18.45
Baptistry and Camposanto open: 08.00-19.40
Leaning Tower open: 08.30-19.20
No children under age 7

FOR THE LEANING TOWER, PRE-BOOK ON 050 560 547. BUY A COMBINED TICKET IF YOU WISH TO SEE ALL THE BUILDINGS.

The visit lasts 30 minutes with a maximum of 35 people allowed at a time. Expect a long queue.

The Tower and the Baptistry of the Campo dei Miracoli are among the most famous images of Italy. The Duomo, finished by Buscheto in 1064, was consecrated by Pope Gelasio II in 1118.

Credit for much of the design and decoration of the buildings in the Campo is given to the Pisano family.

Bonanno Pisano was the first architect for the Leaning Tower, begun in 1173. Taking 200 years to complete, the architecture combines Roman, Gothic and Moorish elements in a flamboyant display of Pisan imagination. It was finished in the second half of the 14th century by Tommaso di Andrea Pisano.

Nicola Pisano (1215-1278) designed the Baptistry and carved the pulpit with scenes from the life of Christ.

Giovanni Pisano contributed the Duomo pulpit.

IT IS OVER 300 STEPS TO THE TOP OF THE TOWER AND IS NOT ADVISABLE FOR PEOPLE WITH HEART PROBLEMS, ASTHMA OR CLAUSTROPHOBIA TO CLIMB THE TOWER.

Pisa Food and Restaurants

Food in Pisa and the surrounding area is delicious, simple and wholesome.

There are some good, reasonably priced restaurants in Piazza delle Tovalglie, which is by day a fish, fruit and vegetable market and by night a general meeting place. One restaurant is set on the ground floor of an old bell tower with limited seating outside.

There are also some great pizzarias dotted around Pisa, often serving *pizza al metro* ('by the metre', meaning you may purchase a slice cut to order).

The current trend in Pisa is *un aperativo* (aperitifs). Some of the main bars include complimentary snacks like *bruschetta*, paté, crisps, olives and tasty cheeses. This is usually really good, well prepared food.

Italian nightlife starts much later than in the UK. People start going out to clubs at about 11pm when we in the UK are all coming home. Having an *apertivo* gives people an opportunity to meet and go out earlier, around 7 pm.

Ice Cream

The best ice cream shop is the Bottega del Gelato in Piazza Garibaldi. It is easy to spot by the queues that form outside it every day, especially in the evenings.

The Regatta

Italy had four ancient maritime powers: Pisa, Genova, Amalfi and Venice. Every year these four cities take it in turns to host an historic regatta. It is great fun as everyone sits along the walls of the river and on the bridges to get the best view of the finish line. In 2002, Amalfi won with Pisa a very close second.

Guigno Pisano

June is a fun time to visit Pisa as it is the *Guigno Pisano* (Pisan June). There are many local festivities.

On *San Ranieri* (Patron Saints' Day) houses along the river bank are given wooden frames to hang on their shutters by the local council. These frames hold candles which are set alight at dusk: the whole city becomes candle lit, with candles floating in the river. The city centre is closed to traffic, to enable people to wander the streets.

Around midnight there is a massive fireworks display over the river: always very impressive and pretty.

Santa Maria della Spina

Lungarno Gambacorti
050 532 474
by appointment only
map D3

Legend has it that it brings bad luck to students if they look at the *Chiesa della Spina* (Church of the Bones) on the day of their examinations. Since most buses from the station go past the church don't be surprised if the students on board suddenly look in the other direction.

It was built to house a holy relic: a thorn from Christ's crown -- returned booty from the Crusades.

The church is rarely open, but the architecture and sculpture of the outside, both the shape and the facade, are worth seeing. Andrea Pisano's *Christ and the Apostles* are in the niches facing the streets.

Look across the languidly curving Arno with its graceful line of yellow ochre and burnt siena buildings providing a contrast to the sparkling white marble of the church.

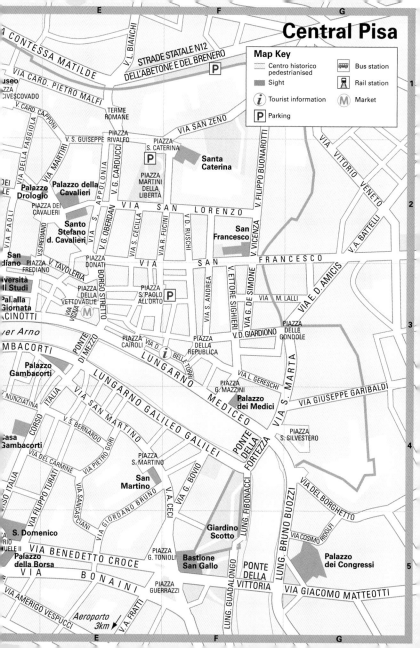

Central Pisa

Map Key

- Centro historico pedestrianised
- Sight
- Tourist information
- Parking
- Bus station
- Rail station
- Market

VIA CONTESSA MATILDE

VIA CARD. PIETRO MALFI

STRADE STATALE N12 DELL'ABETONE E DEL BRENERO

VIA SAN ZENO

VIA CARD. CAPPONI

TERME ROMANE

VIA DELLA FAGGIOLA

VIA MARTIRI

V. S. GUISEPPE

PIAZZA RIVALFO

PIAZZA S. CATERINA

Santa Caterina

VIA G. CARDUCCI

PIAZZA MARTINI DELLA LIBERTÀ

Palazzo Drologio

Palazzo della Cavalieri

PIAZZA DEI CAVALIERI

VIA APPOLONIA

VIA S. OBERDAN

VIA SAN LORENZO

VIA FILIPPO BUONAROTTI

VIA VITORIO VENETO

VIA PAOLI

VS FREDIANO

Santo Stefano d. Cavalieri

VIA S. CECILIA

VIA R. FUCINI

V. D. RUSCHI

San Francesco

V. VICENZA

VIA A. BATTELLI

San diano

PIAZZA FREDIANO

V. TAVOLERIA

PIAZZA DONATI

VIA SAN FRANCESCO

V. ETTORE SIGHIERI

V. G. DE SIMONE

VIA M. LALLI

VIA E. D. AMICIS

versità l Studi

BORGO STRETTO

PIAZZA DELLA VETTOVAGLIE

PIAZZA S. PAOLO ALL'ORTO

V. S. ANDREA

PIAZZA DELLE GONDOLE

Pal. alla Giornata CINOTTI

VIA MADRID

er Arno

MBACORTI

PONTE DI MEZZO

PIAZZA CAIROLI

VIA D.

PIAZZA DELLA REPUBBLICA

V. D. GIARDIONO

BELLE TORRI

VIA S. MARTA

Palazzo Gambacorti

LUNGARNO MEDICEO

LUNGARNO GALILEO GALILEI

PIAZZA G. MAZZINI

VIA L. GERESCHI

VIA GIUSEPPE GARIBALDI

NUNZIATINA

CORSO ITALIA

VIA SAN MARTINO

V. S. BERNARDO

Palazzo dei Medici

PIAZZA S. SILVESTERO

asa Gambacorti

VIA DEL CARMINE

VIA PIETRO GORI

PIAZZA S. MARTINO

V. A. CECI

V. G. BOVIO

PONTE DELLA FORTEZZA

LUNG. BRUNO BUOZZI

VIA DEL BORGHETTO

SO ITALIA

VIA FILIPPO TURATI

VIA SANCASCIANI

VIA GIORDANO BRUNO

San Martino

LUNG. FIBONACCI

VIA COSIMO RIDOLFI

S. Domenico

RIO UELE II

Palazzo della Borsa

VIA BENEDETTO CROCE

PIAZZA G. TONIOLI

Giardino Scotto

Palazzo dei Congressi

VIA BONAINI

Bastione San Gallo

PONTE DELLA VITTORIA

LUNG. GUADALONGO

VIA GIACOMO MATTEOTTI

VIA AMERIGO VESPUCCI

PIAZZA GUERRAZZI

V. A. FRATTI

Aeroporto 3km

TUSCANY COAST

Forte dei Marmi

The glitterati flock to this seaside resort just inside the Tuscany border, an hour south of Portofino. The beach here is long and wide, the sand soft and golden. There are 96 beach clubs, from Bagno Peiro at one end to Bagno Stella Maris at the other. Every one of them rakes and fluffs the sand for perfect sun worshipping. Renting a couple of beds, a parasol and towels from one of these clubs may be expensive but you will be rewarded with a large amount of personal space and little noise.

Forte dei Marmi is currently fashionable. An endless *passiaggiata* of the glitterati dressed in Prada, Gucci and Versace give the resort glamour, Italian style.

This was once a working port, shipping marble to the world. It was discovered back in the 1920s by writers Thomas Mann and Aldous Huxley: *Crome Yellow* and *Antic Hay* were written in a rented house near here. Huxley wrote that living in Forte dei Marmi was like living in a poem by Shelley (who tragically died in a boating accident off the coast of Livorno).

Pietrasanta

The word Pietrasanta means Holy Stone. The town certainly lives up to its name: Michelangelo lived and worked here, while his marble was quarried high in the mountains. Marble used for his *Pieta*, and his *David*. The copies of *David* in Florence where carved in Pietrasanta and in summertime the town is full of stone carvers.

Take a stroll through the charming streets and visit studios where you can purchase your own copy of the *David* or a *Venus de Milo*. Relax at the Bar Michelangelo and listen to the sounds of artisans' hammers and chisels.

PIETRASANTA IS RECOMMENDED FOR ANYONE INTERESTED IN SCULPTURE.

Viareggio

One of the best seaside resorts in Tuscany, Viareggio has wide beaches covered in a honey-coloured sand that is soft on the feet, but firm enough for walking along miles of uninterrupted beach. Excellent cuisine and an exciting nightlife make Viareggio a favourite holiday resort for Italians, German and English tourists. There are many sporting activities to choose from: sailing, windsurfing, horse riding, skating, mini golf and *bocce*. Viareggio has nightclubs, discotheques, restaurants, bars, cafès, pizzerias and ice cream shops.

Beaches

Most of the beaches have been developed as a series of bathing establishments which belong either to a hotel, a commercial interest, or are privately owned. Establishments called *Stabilimenti* or simply *Bagni* usually consist of a connected range of bathing cabins arranged around a central fountain or garden. They are responsible for the cleaness and maintenance of the beach.

The entrance fee covers the hire of an umbrella and deckchairs. When you have rented your umbrella it will be opened for you and it's yours for the day. You may leave it at your leisure and go walking along the beach (or for something to eat), knowing that you have reserved your space on the beach.

DO NOT SIT UNDER AN OPEN UMBRELLA AS IT HAS ALREADY BEEN RENTED.

On hot summer days when the beach is likely to be busy, it is a good idea to select your umbrella early and pay for the rental to reserve your spot on the beach. The public part of the beach is nearer the tide line where there are no umbrellas or beach chairs.

Giro D'Italia

The *Giro D'Italia* is the first of the three Grand Tours of cycling held from mid-May to June 1st. The *Tour de France* follows in July and the *Vuelta* in September.

In 2002, the Giro was the longest of the three at 3,334 kms; the *Tour de France* the shortest at 3,282 kms. The Giro leader, the cyclist in the lead, wears the distinctive pink jersey to signify his status.

The 85th Giro D'Italia (2001) averaged 166 kms per day and featured more climbing with three mountain-top finishes. This race was unusual in that it started outside Italy to celebrate the general introduction of the euro. The race began in Groningen, Netherlands on May 11th and was run over 20 stages through the Netherlands, Belgium, Luxembourg and France before entering Italian soil on May 17th for stage five.

The early stages are suited to the sprinters with the first hilly stage coming in stage six from Cuneo to Varazze, which includes the *Bric Berton* and the *Sassello* climbs.

The seventh stage is a relatively short circuit around Viareggio and Forte dei Marmi along the Tuscany coast, followed by 224 kilometres from Capannori to Orvieto.

Two more flat stages follow before the first mountain finish at Campitello Matese. Corvara to Folgaria is regarded as the hardest stage of the Giro and goes over the Bondone and up the hard side of Santa Barbara (which is a very steep, tough climb) before finishing with the ascent of Folgaria.

The sprinters get a couple more chances before the finale in Milan.

Boat Building

Viareggio has a large pleasure craft harbour and many thriving custom boatbuilding/restoration family businesses. Some have been handed down over five generations. The town also has a large daily fish market supplying restaurants as far away as Florence and Siena.

It is also possible to buy a small, mass-produced craft of little more than three metres, a wooden sailing boat for the passionate sailor, or a luxury yacht with the appropriate gold fittings.

Pisa had navigation and scientific knowledge, Genoa had craftsmen with an aptitude for designing fast ships. It was the Genoese who designed the Caravele, fast sailing vessels used by the Portugese to navigate round the southern tip of Africa and on to India and China.

Sailing crafts have been designed and built on this stretch of the Mediterranean coast for centuries. Viareggio has a reputation for quality and design and businesses here have prospered thanks to the new demand for luxury yachts by post-war high-income consumers. The simplicity and low cost of fibreglass construction fuelled a boat building boom in the 1960s and 1970s.

Renowned shipyards that can claim over a century of experience are: Codecasa, Benetti, Picchiotti, Perini and San Lorenzo. CUV yards are the heirs to Maria dei Medici's *Capitana Nuova*. Alongside the actual builders is a vast and fragmented service sector supplying manufacturers and consumers with every service imaginable: design, repairs, maintenance, insurance, import-export and brokerage, various port harbour services, chartering and other tourist services.

To charter a boat ask the concierge at your hotel, visit the local Tourist Information Office, or ask your tour operator's representative.

Beach Safety

A first aid service is supplied to bathers by qualified lifeguards in every bathing establishment.

Flags are used to communicate sea conditions:

Red flag   Danger
Yellow flag   No Lifeguard
White flag   No Danger

Watersports

A variety of watersports are available along the beach. Enquire at establishments.

Bicycles

May be hired from your hotel, or in the pinewood in Viareggio or by the pier in Forte dei Marmi.

Golf
Forte dei Marmi

Versilia Golf Club
Via Ignazio Da Carrara, 83,
058 488 1574

Tennis

Tennis courts and equipment can be hired by the hour
Viareggio:
Italia Viale Buonarroti
Pinta de Ponente (pinewood)
Forte dei Marmi:
Tennis Europa, Via Colombo

Rollerblading

In the Pineta de Ponente, pine wood in Viareggio.

Horse Riding
Viareggio:
Societa Ippica Viareggio
Pineta di Levante
Marina di Pietrasanta:
Managgio La Versiliana Parco della Versiliana

Beach Shopping

Most shops are open in the mornings from 09.00–12.30 or 13.00 and later in the afternoon from 16.00–19.30 or 20.00.

During the low season, shops are closed on Monday mornings. In high season, shops along the promenade in Viareggio are open later. In the town centre in Forte dei Marmi shops open again in the evening from 21.00–22.30.

Supermarkets

There is a Supermercato in Viareggio on the Promenade and a Conad market on the Via Fratti near the hospital behind the pine wood. It is open till 20.00 and closed on Mondays in the low season. The supermarket in Forte dei Marmi is a long walk away from the hotels in Via Nenni and is open 08.30-13.00, 15.30-19.00 Monday-Saturday.

Buses

Bus stops are labelled with the company that runs the service.

CLAP runs from Viareggio to Forte Dei Marmi, stopping at the towns between.
LAZZI goes to Torre del Lago which is the last stop.

Parking

Parking is free of charge between the white parking bays. There is a 'pay and display' system in the blue parking bays or car parks.

After the coins have been inserted into the machine located near the parking bays, the ticket must be displayed on the dashboard. In some areas there is an attendant who will leave a written parking ticket on your windscreen. Pay the attendant when you leave.

Tuscany's mountains

Situated in the northernmost part of Tuscany is a landscape of supreme natural beauty. The Apuan Alps are a magnificent mountain range that has been preserved as a park expert where Tuscany's fine white marble is quarried.

The slopes of the Apuan Alps are sprinkled with charming and ancient villages within easy reach of the coast and many offer breathtaking views. The village of Monteggiori has an ancient Rotaio Castle. Pieve has a church from the 13th century, although the village itself dates from the 9th century. La Culla, Santa Lucia, Vado and Pedona are all delightful spots to stop and wander.

Take a pleasant drive along the Via Proviniciale from Camaiore to Lucca, passing through the scenic Freddana Valley. This area is full of natural beauty; Romanesque churches, ancient farmhouses and watermills, ice-cold streams flowing down from the mountain peaks. From here it is easy to reach the Luccese Valley or the village of Gombitelli, famous for the craftsmanship of wrought iron. In Celle Di Pescaglia is the 16th century home of Puccini's grandparents.

Up in the hills behind Forte dei Marmi is the village of Santa Anna di Stazema, where there is a monument to the 500 women, children and elderly who were executed by the retreating Germans at the end of World War II.

A spectacular view of the whole coastline extends as far as Elba on clear days.

Parco Naturale delle Alpi Apuane

Take the Seravezza turning at Forte Dei Marmi and follow the road over the autostrade and up into the mountains. Soon you will find yourself driving along river valleys through trees dappled with sunlight. Continue towards Castelnuovo as the road climbs higher into the mountains. The Apuane Alps are known for the precious marbles and other decorative and building materials they provide.

If you have a day to explore, a good drive is through the Alpi towards Castelnuovo from the coast, and then follow the Serchio river south towards Lucca. This route will take you through the towns of Barga and Bagni di Lucca, where there is a choice of good restaurants, before ending the day back in Lucca.

For a shorter itinerary, take the turning to Massa at the junction in the middle of the mountains after the very long tunnel. This road has magnificent views of the Alpine Alps and the rolling hills that lead down to the sea and the town of Massa. The road meanders dramatically and there are viewing points where you may stop and take photographs.

Pietro Pellegrini

The botanical gardens were instituted in 1966, in *Pian della Fioba*, in Comune di Massa. Placed in the middle of Alpi Apuane, at an altitude of 900 metres, the gardens offer a comprehensive range of Alpine flora and are open to visitors every day from mid-May to mid-September 09.00-10.00 and 15.00-18.00.

Carrara Marble

Carrara marble is so white it sparkles. In its natural state it looks like snow cascading down a glacier. You can easily pick up a piece and take it home where it will glisten in the light.

Carrara marble has been the favoured marble for sculptors since ancient Rome. Traditional methods of extracting stone has carved the mountain surfaces even at the highest altitude, covering several ridges with debris, *ravaneti,* and creating a unique landscape.

The quarries perch on the sides of mountain peaks. Workers must navigate their flat-bed lorries upwards along narrow winding tracks into the quarry to load with marble which is then driven at full Italian speed down twisting mountain roads to be cut and shipped around the world. Workers in Michelangelo's time went on strike for higher prices several times as the artist was known to be cheap and slow to pay his bills.

Marble Quarries
Colonnata
(8km east of Carrara)
0585 844 403

It is possible to drive directly to areas where marble is being excavated and on to the mountain-top town of Colonnata. Locals say that this little town has been existence since ancient Roman times when the quarries were first cut. Looking down from Colonnata you can see Carrara and, on a clear day, the turquoise blue of the Mediterranean Sea. The main concentration of quarries is found on the slopes by the city of Carrara.

ROADS DOWN TO CARRARA AND MASSA ARE WINDING AND CAN BE DANGEROUS. IF A LORRY OR MOTORCYCLE FOLLOWS TOO CLOSELY TAKE ADVANTAGE OF THE MANY LAY-BYS.

Michelangelo's Road

Seravezza is located at the junction of the rivers Serra and Vezza. It is the starting point of a moderate hike along the ancient road that Michelangelo built to gain access to his marble quarry at Monte Altissimo.

From Seravezza, follow the road along the river Serra towards the direction of Malbacco. After about 1 km the road becomes steep and you can catch a glimpse of Michelangelo's road down in the ravine on your left. The ancient road meets the modern, near a cement powerline across the road from a small carpark.

Michelangelo's road has a stone wall flanking the ravine side at the starting point. The sections used to transport the marble blocks down the mountain are still visible and stones bear the marks of wagon wheels.

The trail gradually makes its way to Malbacco, an aquamarine pool surrounded by white marble boulders and fed by a shaft of water shooting down the mountainside. This is the local swimming hole so be sure to bring your bathing suit for a refreshing reward.

Barga

Leonardo enjoyed spending plenty of his time in this beautiful town at the foot of the Garfagnana mountains. The palm trees, pleasant climate and lack of insects made it popular with the Medici who granted Barga their protection. The ceramicist Andrea della Robbia liked Barga and his works can be seen throughout the town.

Barga comes to life in the summer with several festivals including: Opera, Jazz, Art and a special town festival.

ASSISI

Assisi

The atmosphere around Assisi is very difficult to put into words. It is the birthplace of St Francis, patron saint of Italy, and is one of the most visited places in the world. Yet Assisi manages to retain a feeling of peace and tranquility amid the souvenir shops and tourist tack. The spirit of St Francis seems to be present, especially in the early dawn hours, and at dusk when the coaches have departed and Assisi's children play football in front of the many churches connected to the life of the great saint.

Francis is patron saint for birds, ecology, environment and animal welfare groups, zoos, lace-makers, tapestry workers and San Francisco, California. He has been dead almost a thousand years, yet millions of people visit the Basilica San Francesco every year and numbers are increasing. One might assume that the attraction is the Giotto fresco cycle of *The Life of Saint Francis* in the Upper Chapel, but it's the Saint's tomb in the crypt that is most visited. People come to pay homage, say mass, and then queue to sign away their worldly wealth to the monks seated behind plain wooden desks.

Assisi sits high atop Mount Subasio and commands a view across the fertile Valle Umbria, which is dominated by the dome of the Basilica Santa Maria degli Angeli. The huge church was built to cover *La Porziuncola*: a tiny church where St Francis hid from his father and where the Franciscan Order was born. St Francis died here in 1226; his bones were later moved to his tomb in the Basilica San Francesco. It was a mere two years after his death that Francis was canonised by Pope Gregory IX on 16th July 1228.

St Francis

Francis was the son of Pietro Bernardone of the wealthy Moriconi family. His mother christened him Giovanni but Pietro insisted he be called Francesco (Francis, meaning 'the Frenchman'). This is the only nickname to enter the Litany of Saints.

Pietro was a cloth merchant who travelled to trade fairs. His son was brought up to follow in his footsteps. Francis was taught to speak, read and write in French as well as Umbrian Latin. Pietro indulged his extravagant son: Francis dressed as a prince and was the life of the party.

There was little indication of the direction his life would take, save for one incident when he was twelve and working in his father's shop. A beggar approached and asked for alms. Francis impatiently refused but the beggar had not gone far when he caught up to him, vowing that he would never again refuse a request made in the name of God.

In the wars of the Guelph and the Ghibelline, Assisi supported the Guelphs while Perugia was Ghibelline. In 1197, Francis dutifully marched out with the citizen army against Perugia and was captured. While prisoner, Francis kept up a consistent gaiety that lightened the spirits of his fellow captives and boasted that he could '*see the day when the whole world will do me homage*'. This was remembered 30 years later when his prophesy came true.

When peace was established, Francis returned home where he fell ill. He began to suspect the material benefits of the temporal world. Having recuperated, he soon forgot his thoughts and left for war again, declaring that someday he would become a great prince.

Pietro had purchased the latest state-of-art knightly armour for Francis. He had only got as far as Spoleto on the long road south to Rome when he had a vision and heard a voice asking: 'Francis, whom is it better to serve, the Lord or the servant?'

'Surely it is better to serve the Lord,' said Francis.

'Why then dost thou make a Lord of the servant?'

'Lord what dost Thou wish me to do?' Francis asked. He was told to return home where he would learn God's will. Francis returned home a changed man. He continued to be extravagant, but now it was all for God: nothing was too beautiful or costly for the service of God. His mission had begun.

The Giotto cycle of frescoes in the Basilica illustrate stories from Francis's life. Number four shows him kneeling before the crucifix in the chapel of San Damiano. Here God is telling him to repair the church building. To finance the works, Francis sold Pietro's goods and then had to face his father in court. There Francis ripped off his garments and laid them at Pietro's feet. Standing naked, he renounced his father and his wealth.

Giotto's fresco humorously depicts the Bishop's expression as he wraps Francis in his own cloak. There is no evidence that father and son were ever reconciled. A rough workman's tunic, with a length of rope as a belt, is the dress of the Franciscan monks. Francis declared that he was wedded to Lady Poverty, *'the most beautiful and desirable and beloved lady.'*

Francis began to attract followers who publicly gave away their possessions to follow Francis at a time when papal clerics lived in splendour and had considerable wealth and influence, often extracting payment from the faithful for the forgiveness of sins. Francis declared that his followers should perform menial tasks to earn their keep; eat what they were given in return for their services; beg when they had nothing; sleep anywhere possible; shun material comforts.

This dramatic appeal to the gospel spread throughout Assisi and many young men left their families and homes causing widespread criticism for throwing perfectly good citizens 'homeless and penniless' on the world. The Bishop called Francis to account but he answered: *'My Lord if we keep property we shall need arms to defend ourselves, and we shall be constantly involved in litigation and feuds; and this will often prevent us from loving God and our neighbour. Therefore we desire to possess no temporal goods in this world'.* The Bishop agreed and interceded with Pope Innocent to gain an audience for Francis.

Pope Innocent refused to see Francis, but then had a dream that a beggar was supporting the tottering church on his shoulder. He summoned Francis and his companions to the papal court to present his arguments. Cardinal John responded, *'If we reject the petition of this poor man, as being new and too hard to fulfill when all he asks is that the law of the Gospel be confirmed to him, let us beware that we do not offend the Gospel of Christ.'* Pope Innocent gave his blessing.

The brothers needed a home and *La Porziuncola* was offered by the Benedictine abbot of San Benedetto, on the condition that it should always be considered the mother church of the order. The tiny chapel is now inside the large Basilica de Santa Maria degli Angeli, which was built to protect the tiny Franciscan church.

Thousands travelled to Assisi to hear Francis speak. Among those listening was Clare, the daughter of a nobleman, challenged, she took a vow of poverty at the altar of the Porziuncola. Francis cut off her long hair and she put on the rough habit of poverty and the white veil of chastity. Her enraged family came for her but Clare defended herself by clinging to the altar. When they saw her shorn hair they left her alone. A Franciscan order of the Poor Clares, or *Pauvre Chiara* was formed.

Francis loved animals and enjoyed a special relationship with them. It is said he once stilled a multitude of birds who listened attentively while he preached. He also tamed a wolf that had long been terrifying the people of Gubbio. Stories about him spread: many frescoes throughout Italy depict scenes of St Francis with birds and animals.

Francis travelled widely preaching the Gospel, even to muslims in Palestine. Franciscan brothers went on missions across Europe spreading the word and increasing their numbers. After a time, the Brothers asked Francis to allow the Order to accumulate some possessions and live in houses. Francis refused, saying that the Oath of Poverty was dictated to him by Christ. He resigned from the Franciscans in 1221. Francis received the stigmata while in meditation on Mount Alvernia in 1224. It continued to bleed sporadically until the time of his death two years later in 1226.

Let us also love our neighbours as ourselves. Let us have charity and humility. Let us give alms because these cleanse our souls from the stains of sin. Men lose all the material things they leave behind them in this world, but they carry with them the reward of their charity and the alms they give. For these, they will receive from the Lord the reward and recompense they deserve. We must not be wise according to the flesh. Rather we must be simple, humble and pure. We should never desire to be over others. Instead, we ought to be servants who are submissive to every human being for God's sake. The Spirit of the Lord will rest on all who live in this way and persevere in it to the end. He will permanently dwell in them. They will be the Father's children who do his work.

Letter from St Francis to the faithful

Basilica di San Francesco

075 819 001
06.30–18.00 daily, November to Easter
06.30–19.00 Monday–Friday, Easter to November
closed Sunday morning and public holidays
Giotto frescoes 08.30-18.00 daily

The Basilica is divided into two levels; the lower church with relics of St Francis and the crypt containing the coffin of the saint; and the upper church with a series of 28 frescoes depicting the life of St Francis by Giotto and Cimabue. Attached to the Basilica is the Francisan monastery founded in 1206. The brothers still wear the same garment; brown robe, rope belt and sandals.

The Giotto cycle, The Life of Saint Francis

1 *Francis honoured by beggar*
2 *Francis gives his cloak*
3 *Francis dreams of a palace filled with arms*
4 *Francis prays before crucifix of St. Damian*
5 *Renouncement of wealth*
6 *The dream of Innocent III.*
7 *Rule of the Minor Friars receives oral approbation.*
8 *The chariot of fire.*
9 *Heavenly throne reserved for Francis.*
10 *Devils are cast out of Arezzo.*
11 *St Francis before the sultan.*
12 *The ecstasy of St Francis*
13 *The nativity scene at Greccio.*
14 *The miracle of the spring.*
15 *The preaching to the birds.*
16 *Death of the knight of Celano.*
17 *Francis before Pope Honorius*
18 *Francis appears at Arles*
19 *Francis receives the stigmata.*
20 *The death of St Francis*
21 *Agostino and the Bishop*
22 *The confirmation of the stigmata.*
23 *The farewell of the nuns of St. Clare*
24 *Canonization of St. Francis*
25 *The apparition to Gregory IX*
26 *The healing of John.*
27 *The woman brought back to life.*
28 *The liberation of Peter.*

Basilica di Santa Chiara
0758 122 82
06.30–12.00, 14.00–19.00
closed 18.00 in winter
Shrine of San Damiano
10.00-18.00 daily
The church of St Clare also
has frescoes by Giotto. The
Chapel of the Crucifix off
the south side of the nave
contains relics of St Francis
and the painted crucifix
which spoke at San Damiano.

Chiesa Nuova
This church was founded on
the remains of the birthplace
of St Francis. Ask the guide
to show you the shop where
Pietro sold his fabrics.

Rocca Maggiore
The castle is at the very top of
Assisi and from here there is a
beautiful view over the town
and valley.

Basilica della Porziuncola
Piazza della Porziucola
0758 051 430
09.00-12.30, 15.00-18.30
closed Sundays

Treasury of the Basilica, Perkins collection
0758 190 01
09.30-12.00, 14.00-18.30
closed Sunday
closed November to March
Illuminated manuscripts, gold
icons and other treasures.

Eremo delle Carceri
4km from Assisi.
The Hermitage is where St
Francis and his followers
came to pray and meditate.
The cloister building and
simple chapels, located in
an oak forest, are in perfect
harmony with the picturesque
mountain landscape.

Basilica di S.Maria degli Angeli, La Porziuncola

075 80 511
06.15-20.00, 21.00-23.00 in August

The most striking feature of the plain below Assisi is the dome of the Basilica Santa Maria degli Angeli, one of the largest religious buildings in Christendom. Inside, you will find one of the smallest churches, La Porziuncola, the cradle of the Franciscan Order.

The interior is bright and spacious in keeping with its function to preserve the most important Franciscan symbols and to shelter pilgrims coming to La Porziuncola for prayer. The little Porziuncola is overwhelmed by the huge Basilica in size, but it dominates it in meaning and symbols for the Franciscan movement throughout the world.

In 1216 the Pope recognised the church as an Indulgence; all pilgrims who enter it will be forgiven their sins.

Inside the church is the Capella del Transito built on the site where St Francis died in 1226. At the time it was an infirmary built next to the church for the aid of pilgrims. Above the door is a fresco *Domenico Bruschi* and inside is a terra cotta of St Francis by Andrea della Robbia.

Museo di Basilica di S. Maria Degli Angeli

Piazza Porziuncolaone
0758 051 430
09.00–12.00,15.00-18.00
April-October
closed November-March

FOOD & WINE

Tuscan Cuisine

Simplicity and the freshness of ingredients define Italian cuisine. There is a strong emphasis on meat and, in Tuscany, on the so-called *Cucina Povera,* or poor man's cuisine.

Italians start the day with a light breakfast of espresso or caffe llatte and a pastry. Lunch is substantial, with a first course of pasta or rice, a second course of meat or fish and vegetables, followed by fruit and coffee. The evening meal is served late, around nine. Desserts are reserved for Sunday or feast day, though it is common to have an ice cream during *passegiata.*

When eating out, Italians tend to have three courses. A meal consists of *antipasto* (starter), *primi* (first course) and *secondi* (second course). With the second course they may also add a *contorno* (side plate, vegetables or salad). Normally the main course will not come with vegetables so they have to be ordered separately.

Italian cuisine relies on the quality of fresh vegetables, pure olive oil, range-fed meat, poultry and game, all seasoned with locally grown herbs. Tuscan cooking takes in a wide variety of textures and flavours, but it is rarely excessively piquant and never bland. Tuscan food is designed to go with Tuscan wine, Chianti.

Some of the ingredients are prized and expensive, but several of the best-known and tastiest dishes are based on leftovers. These are improvisations from the days when Tuscan housewives could not afford to let anything go to waste. Many dishes still make use of ingredients such as stale bread which is toasted and rubbed with raw garlic and tomatoes, then doused in olive oil to make *bruschetta.*

Most Florentines have a strong liking for salt in their diet. Bread served with meals is likely to have been made without salt as there is enough in the cooking itself.

Vegetables play an important part in Tuscan cooking. They may appear as *antipasti* or *sott'olio* (preserved in oil) or *sott'aceto* (preserved in vinegar). Many pasta sauces are based on vegetables, and lettuce and greens are combined with oil and vinegar to make delicious salads. Try a hearty omelette containing potato, artichokes or courgettes and sample some of the excellent mushrooms, *funghi porcini.*

Pasta does not dominate the Tuscan diet as much as in the south: *risotto, gnocchi* (a potato pasta) and *polenta* (cornmeal) are delicious alternatives.

Grilled meat over a wood fire is favoured by the Tuscans as are meats roasted on the spit. *Baccala* is a salted cod normally cooked in garlic and served with a tomato sauce or fresh salad.

Tuscany produces various types of cheese. The most popular is *pecorino,* made from sheep's milk. The best of these come from the region around Siena. Try *Pecorino di Pienza*, a cheese that is mild and soft when young, but when coated with oil, ash or tomato paste and then aged creates a hard and flavourful mature cheese.

Restaurants are commonly called either *trattoria* or *ristorante*. A trattoria will serve a more basic, less expensive cuisine while a ristorante is more up-market. However, these distinctions are becoming blurred as home-style cooking gains popularity.A traditional trattoria has no written menu or bottled wine, the diner is given a choice of three daily specials and a jug of the house wine. These are more common in rural areas. Ristorantes always have a menu and a choice of wines.

Antipasti

Antipasto Toscano
Slices of ham, salami, other cold meats and paté served on little pieces of toasted bread, *crostini*, and garlic bread with olive oil, *bruschetta*.

Prociutto crudo con melone
Parma ham with fresh melon.

Primi

Pasta e fagioli
Pasta and beans in a wholesome soup.

Ribollita & Minestrone
A vegetable-based soup with carrots, beans and the famous Tuscan black cabbage, thickened with chunks of bread.

Tris di Pasta
Three types of pasta with different sauces.

Pappardelle alle lepre
Wide ribbon pasta with stewed hare sauce.

Secondi

Bistecca alla Fiorentina
The secret of this steak is the cut of meat which is a speciality of Florence. It is the T-bone cut of Chianina beef: cut very thick (1 ½ inches), grilled over charcoal and wood and always served rare with olive oil, salt and occasionally rosemary. Check the price when ordering, as some restaurants charge by the 100 gramme. When the steak is cooked properly and rested before serving it tastes tender and juicy without being too raw. Asking for a *Fiorentina* well done is taken as an insult.

Tripe Florentine style
Florentines have always been fond of tripe, a humble but tasty food, frequently mentioned since the 15th century in burlesque poetry praising taverns.

Porchetta allo spiedo
Suckling pig on the spit, often served during festivals.

Cinghiale
Wild boar is a specialty of Umbria.

Contorni

Fagioli al olio
White beans in olive oil.

Pinzimonio
Seasoned carrots, fennel, celery and artichokes .

Fagiolini in umido
Runner beans in a tomato sauce.

Dolci

Tiramisu
A sponge biscuit and creamy mascarpone dessert topped with chocolate and often made with liqueur.

Vinsanto con cantuccini
Hard almond biscuits dipped in dessert wine.

Torta della nonna
Pastry base with almond paste and nuts.

Stracchino
Strawberries and whipped cream liquidized and frozen.

Paying your bill

A cover charge usually appears on every restaurant bill. The amount charged varies with the establishment but it is usually €2 per person. If service is not included, it is recommended to leave a 10 per cent tip.

To eat your meal in a hurry and then dash from the table would horrify an Italian. Therefore don't expect your bill or your food to be served with speed. You will need to ask for the bill because bringing it without your approval is considered rude.

In a busy pizzeria it is acceptable to pay at the cash register. In city centre cafes expect to pay for your cappucinno at the cash register before getting your coffee. Place your receipt on the bar and wait to be served.

Restaurant Listings

Restaurants are listed alphabetically according to price range which is signified by the € symbol. Prices are per person including wine and coperto.

€€€€ €75 and over
€€€ €40 - €75
€€ €20 - €40
€ €20 and under

WAITER IN A COUNTRY TRATTORIA

Florence

Florence is a city of trattorias and the best are usually the traditional family-run establishments. Décor is simple: bottles of wine line the walls, wooden or marble-topped tables with unmatching wooden chairs for seating.

This is the heart of Chianti and the *enoteca*, wine bar, has caught on and developed. Enotecas are to Florence what pubs are to London: a great place to meet friends and have fun. Snacks are often available throughout the day.

Residential addresses in Florence are blue and larger than business addresses which are small and red in colour. The letter 'r' after the number indicates a business address. Florentine streets often have two buildings of each address number: one blue and one red.

The average trattoria in Florence is often quite good if one avoids the main tourist areas. Find a restaurant you like and return there often: soon you'll be familiar and offered special off-the-menu items.

Florentines don't generally eat fish and the only dish you are likely to find on the traditional menu is baccala alla livornese: salt cod cooked in garlic and tomato sauce.

The shady piazza in front of Santa Spirito has two good restaurants owned by the same partners, Borgo Antico and Osteria Santo Spirito. Cabiria is a good spot for an aperitivo in the summer when the piazza becomes an open-air bar where musicians sometimes play.

Cibreo

Via del Verrocchio 8r
055 234 1100
13.00–14.30, 19.00–23.15 daily
closed August
credit cards accepted
booking advisable
map G3
€€€€

Fabio Picchi and his wife Benedetta Vitali opened Cibreo in 1979, dedicated to reviving the ancient peasant cooking of Tuscany. The restaurant now has an international reputation. However, be prepared for the eccentricities of your host. The dining experience is unique: a waiter sits down with you to recite the long menu in Italian and English and you may find yourself sharing a large table with other diners. The food is sublime but beware what you order for *secondi*: Picchi loves to challenge his unsuspecting diners. Try the white fish or the roast pigeon and all of the desserts are delicious. The wine list is expensive but you can select a less costly Chianti from the da Vinci collective.

Zibibbo

Via di Terzollina 3r
Careggi
055 433 383
12.30–15.30, 19.30–24.00 daily
closed August
credit cards accepted
booking advisable
off map
€€€€

Benedetta Vitali divorced Fabio, left Cibreo, and opened her own restaurant in Florence's suburb Careggi. It is worth the effort of a bus or taxi journey to dine in Benedetta's modern décor, full of skylights and contemporary Tuscan landscapes. Zibibbo integrates Sicilian cuisine with Middle Eastern cooking, combining flavours not usually found in Tuscan restaurants.

Pane e Vino

Via di San Niccolo 7or
055 247 6956
20.00–23.30 Monday–Saturday
closed August
credit cards accepted
booking advisable
map F5
€€€

Elegant and intimate dining by candlelight, this is the place to come for that special celebration. Try the gnocchi with porcini mushroom *primi* followed by tender lamb chops with fennel and sage. Desserts tend towards the light and fluffy. The wine list features a good selection of Tuscan reds and assorted bottles line the shelves. Service is discreet if slow.

Al Antico Ristoro di Cambi

Via Sant'Onofrio 1r
055 217 134
12.00-14.30, 19.30-22.30
Monday-Saturday
closed August 15
credit cards accepted
booking advisable
off map
€€

If you want the best *bistecca* in Florence, take a taxi to the San Frediano neighbourhood to this friendly trattoria. Try a *primi* of pasta with fresh ricotta and arugula while waiting for your perfectly grilled *secondi* of steak, which is why all the other diners have come here. Order a bottle of Chianti from the bar as the house wine is not up to standard.

Boccadama

Piazza Santa Croce 25-26r
055 243 640
08.30-24.00 daily
closed Monday afternoon
credit cards accepted
booking advisable
map F4
€€

A casual and pleasant atmosphere, Boccadama offers Tuscan cooking to compliment an excellent wine list where the food is created to match the wine. Start with Piedmont Chardonnay and bruschetta with fresh tomato and basil followed by a Tuscan Sangiovese accompanied by potato ravioli topped with wild boar. If you have room for dessert, the chocolate cake, *torta al cioccolato,* is excellent.

Trattoria Cibreo or Cibreino

Via dei Macci 122r
055 234-1100
13.00-15.30, 19.00-23.15
Tuesday-Saturday
closed August
no credit cards
bookings not accepted
map G3
€€

The small trattoria version of the famous Ristorante Cibreo has a more relaxed atmosphere (and price) yet the two share a kitchen with many of the same menu items on offer. The kitchen is known for innovative cooking of traditional Tuscan dishes and they make a splendid flourless chocolate cake.

Trattoria Baldovino

Via San Giuseppe 22r
055 241 773
11.30-14.30, 19.00-23.30 daily
credit cards accepted
booking advisable
map F4
€€

Scottish restauranteur David Gardner also owns the Enoteca Baldovino next door and Beccofino across the Arno. Gardner knows how to please those with particular tastes. The menu is broad and varied serving *focaccia*, pizza, pastas and salads along with more hearty stews and meat dishes. The extensive wine list features plenty of choices of Chianti and wines from other regions. The service is uneven and the noise level can become deafening.

Quattro Leoni
Piazza della Passera
Via Vellutini 1r
055 218 562
11.45-14.30, 19.30-23.00 daily
credit cards accepted
booking advisable
map C4
€€

This unassuming little trattoria is one of the best in Florence and is located in Oltrarno, not far from the Pitti Palace. The food is consistently good, the prices fair and the atmosphere welcoming and comfortable. Pasta and grilled meats dominate the menu, but the preparation and combination of flavours offer a fresh approach to Tuscan cuisine.

Borgo Antico
Piazza Santo Spirito 6r
055 210 437
12.00-15.00, 19.00-23.00 daily
booking advisable
credit cards accepted
map B4
€€

The large shaded patio under the trees in Piazza Santo Spirito is a good place to enjoy a long Italian lunch. Food takes second place to the atmosphere, which is lively and young. Try the linguine with clams or the risotto with stracchino cheese and zucchini flowers. Pizza is made in the wood-fired oven and the portions tend to be large. Service is friendly and the waiters don't rush you.

Veccia Bettola
Piazza Torquato Tasso
Via Ariosto 34r
055 224 158
12.00-14.30, 19.30-22.30
closed August, Christmas week
no credit cards
map A4
€€

Located in Oltrarno not far from Santa Maria del Carmine. This friendly old style trattoria is owned by the same family as the Nerbone sandwich bar in the Mercado Centrale. The house pasta, *penne alla Bettola* made with a vodka and tomato sauce, is excellent as is the rigatoni with olives and roasted tomatos. For *secondi*: traditional grilled chops or a well-prepared *bistecca*.

Le Volpi e L'Uva
Piazza dei Rossi 1r off Via Romana
055 239 8132
10.30-20.30 Monday-Saturday
closed August
booking advisable
credit cards accepted
map D4
€

This tiny wine bar just off the Ponte Vecchio is a perfect place to stop and rest one's feet. Sample an outstanding glass of wine at a reasonable price from the ever-changing list on the chalkboard. Owner Giancarlo Cantini seeks out only small, unknown producers from all regions of Italy for wine that is good value. A true bargain hunter, Giancarlo discontinues wines if they raise their prices.

Trattoria Mario
Via Rosina 2r
055 218 550
12.00-15.30 Monday-Saturday
closed August
no credit cards
map D1
€

Arrive early at this popular trattoria located across from the Mercado Centrale. Mario's cooking tastes so good that the locals crowd in at lunchtime, elbow to elbow for *ribollita, bistecca alla fiorentina* and fish on Friday.

Osteria Antica Mescita di San Niccolo
Via di San Niccolo 6or
055 234 2836
19.30-23.00 Monday-Saturday
credit cards accepted
map E5
€

Sit upstairs at this warm and friendly trattoria serving good hearty soups and stews.

Try the wild boar with spices or beef stew with porcini. The house Chianti is good, as is the large selection of reasonably priced wine by the bottle. In summer you can sit outside.

Antica Porta
Via Senese 23r
Porta Romana
055 220 527
19.30-01.00 Tuesday-Sunday
credit cards accepted
off map
€

Outside the Porta Romana on the south side of Florence, this pizzeria is hidden treasure. The tiny frontage is deceptive: there is a large and bustling dining room at the back. Roman style thin-crust pizza is best eaten here and they offer a good variety. Try the delicious pasta: linguine tossed with mussels and clams cooked in garlic and olive oil.

Il Pizzaiuolo
Via dei Macci 113r
055 241 171
19.30-24.00 Monday-Saturday
closed August and Christmas
no credit cards
booking advisable
map G3
€

Across the street from the Sant' Ambrogio market is this comfortable trattoria-style pizzeria that serves some of the best pizza in the centre. The basic *margherita* is simply yet tastefully prepared, order the *quattro formaggi* if you like cheese. Pizzas are large so you may want to share.

Sandwiches and take away

Enoteca Baldovino
Via San Giuseppe 18r
055 234 7220
12.00-16.00, 18.00-24.00 daily
credit cards accepted
map F4

Located near the Santa Croce and across the street from the more expensive Trattoria Baldovino, this casual *enoteca* is a popular lunch spot for tourists. There is a long list of open face sandwiches *crostini* and several large salads to choose from, as well as an abundance of wines by the glass. Service can be a bit slow during peak periods.

Cantinetta dei Verrazzano
Via dei Tavolini 18-20r
055 268 590
08.00-21.00 Monday-Saturday
closed 2 weeks in August
credit cards accepted
map D3

The Cantinetta is a charming bakery and sandwich bar located in the heart of tourist Florence between the Duomo and the Piazza Signoria. Walk through the bakery at the front to the marble topped bar serving Piansa coffee, where they won't charge you extra if you sit down. Lunch is in the small room next door: fantastic focaccia sandwiches are served straight out of the wood-fired oven. The Verrazzano wine on offer is made by the family, grown on their own Chianti vineyards.

I Fratellini
Via dei Climatori 38r
055 239 6096
08.00-19.00 Monday-Saturday
closed some of August
no credit cards
map E5

Stop here for perfect sandwiches: percorino and arugula, goat's cheese and wild boar salami, mozzarella and tomato, accompanied by a small glass of wine or soda. Eat standing on the street leaning against the wall, not an option if your feet hurt.

Nerbone
Mercato Centrale, first floor
055 219 949
07.00-14.00 Monday-Saturday
closed August
no credit cards
map D1

Florence's version of the hamburger is a sandwich made with boiled beef, *bollito*, dunked in the meaty juices *bagnato* or with spicy sauce, *tutte le salse*. Nerbone also serves pasta, salads and a delicious roast chicken sandwich. Proceed first to the cash register and pay for your order before squeezing your way through hungry

Italians to place your order at the sandwich bar. Avoid the crush by arriving before noon.

Hemingway Tea Room
Piazza Piattellina 9r
055 284 781
summer:
midnight-07.00 Tuesday-Friday
11.30-20.00 Sunday
winter:
16.30-01.00 Tuesday-Saturday
credit cards accepted
book for meals
map A4

Monica Meshini and Emma Mantovani started Hemingway out of a passion for chocolate and it has grown into a lively meeting place near Piazza del Carmine. The hot chocolate is divine. Buffet salads and snacks are available throughout the summer nights. The wine list is small but they serve imported beer.

Caffe Italiano
Via della Condotta 56r
055 291 082
08.00-20.00 Monday-Saturday
map D3

An belle-epoque style cafe with dark paneling and crystal chandeliers is a cozy refuge in the centre. There are international newspapers and magazines available to read.

Fiesole

India
Via Gramsci 43a
055 599 900
07.30-22.30 Wed.-Monday
booking advisable
no credit cards
€€

If you are craving a good Indian, catch the number 7 bus near the Duomo and ride all the way up to the main square in Fiesole. The restaurant is a short walk and serves all the standard favourites including papadam, samosas, tandoori, curries and rice biryani. India's atmosphere is romantic with sitar music and lanterns, somewhat akin to eating inside the tent of a grand sultan.

Artimino

Da Delfina
Via della Chiesa 1
055 871 8119
12.30-15.00, 20.30-22.00
Tuesday-Saturday
12.30-15.00 Sunday
no credit cards
€€

It may be at the end of a long and winding road, but this restaurant still manages to be written up in all the magazines. Chef-owner Carlo Cioni has kept his integrity and serves great Tuscan food in a rustic country setting.

Tuscany

Arrezo

Buca di San Francesco
Via Cavour, Piazza San Francesco
next to the Basilica
0575 232 71
Good food in a serene atmosphere.

Antica Osteria L'Agania
Via Mazzini 10
057 253 81
closed Monday
Pleasant and unpretentious with well prepared food.

Taverna del Lago
Via Borbuio 33
Cavriglia, 42 km west of Arezzo
055 961 039
booking advisable
The only building on a beautiful man-made lake surrounded by hills and trees. Try the excellent *spaghetti vongole*.

Bagni di Lucca

La Mora
Via Sesto di Moriano 1748
0583 406 402
Spacious glass-enclosed dining room surrounded by forest. Reviewed in Gourmet magazine. Try the pigeon and superb local wine: rich and dark.

Camaiore

Il Vignaccio
in Santa Lucia above Camaiore
The best *zuppa della frantoiana* and *ribollita* is served in this small restaurant in the mountains.

Carrara

Ninan
Via Lorenzo Bartolini 3
058 574 741
12.00-14.00 daily
19.00-22.00 Monday-Saturday
closed winter Sundays
credit cards accepted
booking necessary
€€€
Chef Marco Garfagnini has turned his grandmother's parlour into a small perfect restaurant with only six tables. Fellow diners must all agree to order the *menu degustazione* which offers a range of Marco's excellent cooking and, depending on the day, could include: sauteed butterfly shrimp antipasti, crunchy gnocchi followed by grilled pigeon breasts and topped off with a milk custard dessert. The wine list is plentiful and the service attentive. Ninan's reputation has spread so be sure to book ahead.

Castellina in Chianti

L'Albergaccio
Via Fiorentina 35
0577 741 042
12.00-14.00 Monday, Friday and
Saturday
19.00-22.00 Monday-Saturday
closed Sunday
closed November
no credit cards
book in summer
The young chefs are
committed to unusual
ingredients and a
combination of flavours such
as ravioli stuffed with salt
cod served on pureed beans,
or wood pigeon *colombaccio*
simmered in wine and clove.

Antica Trattoria La Torre
Piazza del Comune
0577 740 236
lunch and dinner
closed Friday
closed early September
credit cards accepted
English spoken
book for dinner
€€
This trattoria in the heart
of Chianti has been in the
Stiaccini family for over 100
years. The family is generous
and down-to-earth and
so is the food they serve,
hearty pasta and *bistecca alla
fiorentina* accompanied by the
quality house Chianti.

Castelnuovo di Garfagnana

Albergo Ristorante La Baita
Via Prato all'Aia, Corfino
0583 660 084
lunch and dinner
booking advisable
€
This fun and friendly family-
run trattoria serves gnocchi
which is reputed to be the
best in Tuscany.

Colle val d'Elsa

Arnolfo
Via XX Settembre 52
Colle Alta
0577 920 549
12.00-14.00, 19.00-22.00
closed Tuesday and Wednesday
lunch
closed 1-10 August
credit cards accepted
booking necessary
€€€€
A small elegant restaurant
owned by the Trovato
brothers. Gaetano's cooking
combines traditional
Tuscan with south and east
Mediterranean flavours. His
interesting arrangement, of
food on the plate show his
artistic flair. Try the *tortelli*
and the tiny mountain lamb
chops and save room for
zabaglione for dessert.

L'Antica Trattoria
Piazza Arnolfo 23
0577 923 747
12.00-14.00, 19.00-22.00
closed Tuesday
closed end of December
credit cards accepted
booking advisable
€€€
Warm and friendly Tuscan restaurant serving authentic cuisine. The Paradisi family are excellent hosts and Enrico is a wine enthusiast with a vast cellar.

La Speranza
No 541 south from
Colle Val d'Elsa
lunch and dinner
no credit cards
€
A noisy and friendly Tuscan grill that is popular with the locals. The *bistecca* is excellent as are all the grilled meats. The house wine is nicely drinkable.

Cortona

Il Falconiere
San Martino 43
0575 612 679
lunch and dinner
closed winter Wednesdays
closed November
credit cards accepted
English spoken
book for dinner
€€€€
An elegant restaurant set in a grand villa with a garden and outdoor terrace in summer. The cuisine is a creative variation on native Tuscan ingredients including pumpkin pasta and pheasant with rosemary and juniper. Owners Silvia and Riccardo Barracchi have raised the standards since they inherited the property. The food, wine list and service are excellent.

Osteria del Teatro
Via Maffei 2
0575 630 556
lunch and dinner
credit cards accepted
booking advisable
€€
Enjoy an excellent meal in this cosy dining room with walls covered in autographed photographs of famous opera singers and composers including Puccinni and Maria Callas. Try *asparagus risotto* followed by *duck with black olive* and perhaps *tiramisu*.

Castel Girardi
Castel Girardi 61
0575 691 030
lunch and dinner
closed Tuesdays
book in summer
visa/mastercard
€
A modest trattoria with a fabulous view that welcomes children and has a little playground. Pizza, pasta and tasty salads are served along with grilled daily specials.

Forte dei Marmi

Da Lorenzo
Via Carducci 61
0584 874 030
19.00-23.00 daily
12.00-14.30 September-June
closed winter Mondays
closed December, January
credit cards accepted
English spoken
booking required
€€€€

Lorenzo Viani has the gift of hospitality and his elegant restaurant has a lively atmosphere without the usual snobbery. The fish is delicate and very fresh, purchased by Lorenzo at Viareggio's auction. Delicious food and an award-winning wine make Lorenzo's the place to go, so remember to book.

Gaiole-in-Chianti

Badia a Coltibuono
from Gaiole, take SS408 for
5 km, direction Montevarchi
0577 749 031
lunch and dinner
closed Monday
closed January, February
credit cards accepted
booking advisable
€€

Good Tuscan cooking using ingredients grown on the Coltibuono and neighbouring estates. Try *risotto al limone* followed by *bistecca*. The estate wine is excellent and

OSTERIA DEL TEATRO

they offer direct sale of wine, oil, vinegar and other products. Be sure to try their homemade chocolates.

Greve-in-Chianti

Il Vescovino
Via Ciampolo da Panzano 9
Panzano
055 852 464
lunch and dinner
credit cards accepted
booking advisable
€€
Enjoy a long leisurely lunch taking in the panoramic view of the Chianti countryside.

Lucca

La Buca di Sant'Antonio
Via della CerVia 3
0583 558 81
12.30-14.30, 19.30-23.00
Tuesday – Saturday
11.00-15.00 Sunday
credit cards accepted
map C3
€€
Located in a restored 19th century hostelry near San Michele, this restaurant is an institution serving traditional Lucchese cooking. Try *farro all garfagnana*, a thick soup or *tordelli lucchesi*, very large tortelloni for primi and the spit-roasted kid *capretto allo spiedo* for secondo.

Da Guido
Via Cesare Battisti 28
12.00-14.30, 19.30-22.00
Monday – Saturday
credit cards accepted
map D2
€
Good reliable food and a warm welcome from the owners make this trattoria a favourite among locals and tourists alike, serving Lucchese specialties; soup and tortelli, as well as roast rabbit for secondi and a lovely sweet spinach cake for dessert. *Prezzi modicissimi* is the Barsotti brothers' motto meaning prices are kept low.

Da Giulio in Pelleria
Via delle Conce 45
Piazza San Donato
0583 559 48
A large and bustling restaurant serving good food at modest prices.The menu is for tourists, ask the waiter what he suggests. Try porcini mushrooms with polenta, fagioli or bean and barley soup (a Lucchese specialty).

Massa Pisana

Locanda L'Elisa
Via Nuova per Pisa 1952
0583 379 019
€€€€
Now a 5 star hotel, this villa was once owned by Napoleon's sister Elisa

Baciocchi. It has beautiful gardens and a restaurant conservatory. Enjoy a romantic dinner on the Belle Epoque veranda overlooking the park and savour one of the exceptional local vintages.

Montecatani Terme

Enoteca Giovanni
Via Garibaldi 25/27
0572 730 80
lunch and dinner
closed Monday
closed 2 weeks in August
credit cards accepted
booking advisable
€€€€€-€€

Giovanni Rotti is really two establishments: a modern, elegant restaurant serving haute-cuisine on one side and an informal wine bar serving hearty Tuscan dishes on the other. Both benefit from an extensive wine cellar of over 12,000 bottles.

Montefollonico

La Chiusa
Via Madonnina 88
0577 669 668
lunch and dinner
credit cards accepted
booking advisable
€€€€

Serving imaginative cuisine in a romantic setting is the perfect setting for a special celebration.

Montepulciano

La Grotta
opposite San Biagio church
1 km west of Montepulciano
0578 757 607
12.00-14.30, 19.00-22.30
closed Wednesday
closed January, February
credit cards accepted
book for dinner
€€

A spacious dining room with walls of stone and a large fireplace for cooler days and a large shady garden for al fresco summertime eating. The kitchen is a marriage of French and Tuscan, try raviolini stuffed with ricotta mousse and basil followed by rabbit in a sweet and sour sauce. Have a berry tart for dessert.

Caffe Poliziano
Via Voltaia nel Corso 27
0578 758 615
07.00-01.00 daily
credit cards accepted
no bookings
€

This Italian art nouveau café has been a town landmark since 1868. Relax over a café, lunch or an apertivo and enjoy the exceptional view over the valley. There are six primi on offer for lunch and three set-menu dinners.

Ristorante della Frattoria di Pulcino

just outside the walls on the
Chianciano road
0578 758 711
lunch and dinner
no credit cards
€

This large casual restaurant
serves food grown on the
farm, as well as products to
take away. The menu varies
daily depending on the
ingredients available. For
dessert, try the *panello della
Gabriella*, a nut cake made
from an old Franciscan recipe.

Pescia

Ristorante Cecco

Via Forti 96/98
0572 477 955
Lunch and dinner
closed Monday
closed July
and 2 weeks in January
credit cards accepted
booking advised on weekends
€€

The menu features unusual
locally grown jumbo green
asparagus among other
specialties, including
mushrooms which appear
on the menu in early
summer. Try the *gnocci
della cassa* tossed with sliced
porcini mushrooms, shaved
parmesan and wild marjoram,
and follow it with the house
chicken, *pollastrino al mattone*,

cooked on the griddle and
served crispy on the outside
with moist and tender meat
inside.

Pienza

Il Chiostro di Pienza

Corso Rossellinio 26
0578 748 440
lunch and dinner
credit cards accepted
booking recommended
€€€

Delicious Tuscan cooking
served in a restored 15th
century cloister and lit by
candles. Il Chiostro has a fine
wine cellar and view from the
garden.

Trattoria latte di Luna

Via San Carlo 2/4
0578 748 606
12.00-14.00, 18.00-21.30
closed Tuesday
closed February and July
credit cards accepted
booking advisable
€€

A small family-run trattoria
with tables out in the piazza
in the summertime. The
portions are generous and
tasty, try *pici all'aglione* thick
spaghetti in a garlicky tomato
sauce or *formato di zucchine*,
a vegetarian souffle. Meat is
expertly roasted or grilled,
choose from steaks, sausage,
duck and suckling pig. The
wine is a good local variety,
the prices are fair and the
service is friendly.

Pietrasanta

L'Enoteca Marcucci
Via Garibaldi 40
0584 791 962
wine bar
10.00-13.00, 17.00-01.00
restaurant
20.00-24.00
closed winter Mondays
credit cards accepted
booking advisable
€€
The Marcucci brothers run
the Enoteca and offer a
large selection of Italian and
international wines. The
Marcucci parents do all the
cooking for dinner which is
the only meal served. Main
courses can be unusual;
struzzo alla brace, ostrich
grilled over wood embers
is one example . Signor
Marcucci grows all the herbs
and seasonings in his own
garden.

Bar Michelangelo
Piazza Duomo
12.00-24.00
A pleasant place to sip an
apertivo and listen to the
sound of artists at work.

Pisa

Antica Trattoria Il Campano
Via Cavalca 44
050 580 585
lunch and dinner
map E3
€€

Located in a quiet location
by the market. Emphasis on
seafood dishes and pasta.
The narrow terrace is ideal
for dining al fresco in the
summer. Extensive wine list.

Osteria dei Cavalieri
Via San Frediano 16
050 580 858
lunch and dinner
closed Saturday afternoon
closed Sunday
closed August
booking advisable
credit cards accepted
map E2
€€
The menu offers variety and
one-dish specials like mixed
grilled fish with pasta. Good
value for money.

Almatea
Piazza Cairoli
map E3
Enjoy an *aperitivo* beside the
river Arno.

Poggibonsi

La Galleria
Galleria Cavalieri
Vittorio Veneto 20
0577 982 356
lunch and dinner
closed Sunday
closed August
credit cards accepted
English spoken
booking advisable
€€
Don't be put off by the bland
modern exterior of the tower

block that houses La Galleria. Michele Targi and his wife Letizia serve Tuscan food with a creative refinement honed in Florence's best restaurants and they serve a fine selection of fish. Desserts are homemade and lovingly presented, try the Medici pudding.

San Gimignano

Ristorante Dorando
Vicolo dell'Oro 2
0577 941 862
12.00-14.00, 19.00-22.00
closed Monday
booking advisable
credit cards accepted
€€€
One of the better restaurants in a narrow street off Piazza Cisterna, serving creative modern dishes as well as Tuscan traditional cuisine.

Le Terrazze dell'Hotel La Cisterna
Piazza della Cisterna 24
0577 940 328
lunch and dinner
booking advisable
€€€
The hotel restaurant serves high quality Tuscan dishes and has an excellent view.

Ristorante Le Vecchie Mura
Via Piandornella 15
0577 940270
18.00-23.00 daily
closed for lunch

booking advisable
€€
Good Tuscan food served on an outside terrace.

La Mangiatoia
Via Mainardi 2
0577 941 258
lunch and dinner
closed Friday
no credit cards
booking advisable
€€
Tuscan cooking that uses local flavours and wines, try rabbit cooked in Vernaccia wine or the wild boar with walnuts *cinghiale con noci.*

Osteria delle Catene
Via Mainardi 18
0577 941 966
closed Wednesday
closed January
credit cards accepted
€€
Classic Tuscan cooking with some interesting twists such as *straccotto* braised beef in Chianti and *faraona* guinea fowl cooked with juniper.

San Vincenzo

Ristorante Gamero Rosso
Piazza della Vittoria 19
0565 701 021
lunch and dinner
closed Tuesday
closed November
credit cards accepted
booking essential
€€€€

This charming restaurant is famous for its innovative seafood cuisine and features an excellent wine list. The entrance is via a set of stairs connecting the port to the shopping street above. Tables have views of the sea, framed by arched windows facing south west. Owner/chef Fulvio Pierangelini serves Italian cuisine in a French style using fresh ingredients, simply prepared and full of flavour. Try *Passatina di Ceci con Gamberi,* a puree of chick peas with lightly steamed shrimps, followed by squid and turbot ravioli served with a ragout of crayfish. Desserts are light and delectable.

Sanselpolcro

Da Ventura
Via Aggiunti 30
0575 742 560
lunch and dinner
closed Saturday
closed January and August
credit cards accepted
booking advisable
€€
Hot pasta with a choice of sauces are served from a *primi* trolley: diners can choose the pasta, sauce and size of helpings. The trolleys return laden with *secondi* choices and later with a *dolci* selection.

Ristaurante L'Erbhosteria del Castello

Badia Tedalda
Rofelle
0575 714 017
open Sunday lunch
booking necessary
€

Rofelle is a 45 minute drive from Sanselpolcro along the SS258 to Rimini. Follow the signs for Viamaggio and then Badia Tedalda. Turn left at the blue sign for Rofelle just before Baldia Tedalda. Follow the white road to the trattoria. Relax and enjoy a long Italian lunch.

There is no menu and the wine is homemade. The food is exceptional and uses fresh local herbs and flavours. Lunch may consist of several courses and may last many hours so it's advisable to pace yourself. Dishes will vary according to season but some favourites are: crostini with wild mushroom, fresh ricotta cubes with purple wild flowers, wild asparagus with thin cheese and pear quiche antipasti, nettle ravioli, veal with porcini, grilled guinea fowl with truffles and juniper. If you haven't left space for dessert(!), end the meal with a herbal *digestivo*.

Siena

Antica Trattoria Botteganova

Strada Chiantigiana 29 (SS 408)
0577 284 230
12.00-14.30, 18.30-22.00
closed Monday
English spoken
credit cards accepted
book for dinner
€€€€

In a formal atmosphere just outside the city gates, Guido Bellotti and Michele Sorrentino offer two tasty menus in addition to the main menu. The four course menu including wine is good value. The young chef enjoys layering unusual flavours, such as *mazzancolle*, breaded shrimp served on braised onions, . For those less adventurous, the pastas are good as is the grilled *bistecca*.

Osteria le Logge

Via del Porrione 33
0577 480 13
12.00-14.30, 18.00-22.00
closed Sunday
closed end November
booking advisable
map D3
€€€€

Just off the Campo, this is Siena's favourite gathering place for locals and visitors. The atmosphere is not overly formal and in the summer there are tables outside in the street. Vegetables always taste good here, try them with pasta or risotto for a lighter meal. Save room for the crunchy baked pecorino with honey and pine nuts. Owner Gianni Brunelli's Rosso is excellent as is the wine list .

Il Ghibellino
Via dei Pellegrini 26
0577 288 079
12.00-14.30, 18.00-22.00
closed Monday
English spoken
credit cards accepted
book for dinner
map D3
€€
Located between the Campo and the Duomo, this is the perfect place to relax for lunch. The prices are reasonable and food is traditional Tuscan cucina povera; soup or pasta for primi and rabbit or tripe for secondi, fish is available on Thursday and Friday evenings.

Liberamente Osteria
Piazza del Campo 26
0577 274 733
10.00-23.30 Monday-Saturday
closed Sunday
credit cards accepted
booking possible
map D3
€
This sophisticated wine bar is right on the campo and makes a perfect place to enjoy a glass of wine and a snack.

The beautiful interior has been decorated by painter Sandro Chia.

Viareggio

Romano
Via Mazzini 120
0584 313 82
lunch and dinner
closed Monday and January
credit cards accepted
English spoken
booking advisable
€€€€
Romano Franseshini has been operating this restaurant since they were 22 and 16 respectively.. Today all the children work here to provide excellent fish dishes using fresh ingredients from the Viareggio market just a few steps away. The wine list is extensive and features a good selection of white wines. Viareggio is famous for Carnevale and Romano's serves seasonal pastries along with sorbet and a mousse that is light-as-air.

Osteria Barcobestia
Via Coppino 201
058 438 4416
lunch and dinner
credit cards accepted
booking advisable
€€
A simple trattoria that is excellent for fish without being overly expensive.

Chianti

Tuscany's most famous wine is Chianti, the name for wines produced in the region under a regulated formula. Chianti Classico is both a region and a wine: the area where the wine is produced is a hybrid of sections of the provinces of Florence and Siena. The overall area for Chianti production is a larger one, extending into the provinces of Siena and Florence, as well as Pisa, Arezzo and Pistoia.

Chianti, as we know it, was created in the Castello di Brolio, an estate in the hills north-west of Siena. In the 19th century, Baron Nettino Ricasoli, a former Italian prime minister, brilliant, cross-eyed and very jealous, snatched his wife away from a ball in Florence because a young man had made a pass at her. Legend has it that he drove her to the castle and kept her there forever.

The Baron began to experiment with wines and became known as the inventor of modern Chianti. By combining the Sangiovese and Canaiolo grapes, plus a little white Malvasia and Trebbiano, he gave birth to the formula used to make Chianti Classico in 1874. Today, the recipe has changed slightly; now very little or no Trebbiano is added.

Chianti can vary widely from a light, refreshing, inexpensive drink to the full-flavoured, deep red, estate bottled, barrel-aged reserve wine. Between the two extremes lie thousands of different wines, varying in quality, but all based on the Sangiovese grape. Wines are produced by large and small estates; several are owned by Tuscan aristocrats who give their names to some of the finest wines. The descendants of Baron Ricasoli, who still live in Castello di Brolio, produce a fine Chianti under the name *Brolio*.

Wines produced by the *Chianti Classico Consortium* have the symbol of the black cockerel on the label. Along with the *Chianti Rufina* and *Chianti dei Colli Fiorentini*, they have stricter regulations and are often of a better quality than the other Chianti subdivisions.

Chianti may be drunk when young or old; young wine goes into the typical flask, the old into bottles. When aged for at least three years in oak casks it is entitled to the honour *Riserva*.

So-called *Super-Tuscan* wines are made entirely of red grapes, including the foreign Cabernet Sauvignon. These are inspired by the great wines of Bordeaux and are often aged in oak *barriques.*

There are other red wines of distinction in Tuscany, which are close in character to Chianti: *Vino Nobile di Montepulciano, Brunello, Rosso di Montalcino, Carmignano, Sassicaia, Coltassala, I Sodi, Prima Vigna, Sangioveto di Colti-bouno, Solaia* and *Tignanello.*

Traditionally, white wines are not produced in the same quantities as red, but are becoming more popular, especially the ancient *Vernaccia di San Gimignano, Galestro, Torricella* and the Chardonnay wine from the *Tenuta Pomino* of Frescobaldi.

Chianti Vineyards

The area between Florence and Siena has some of the most scenic landscapes in Italy and is known for producing several different types of Chianti. As you travel through the countryside you will see signs with grapes on them that indicate the variety being made.

Chianti Vineyards

There are hundreds of vineyards and wine estates in the area. Wherever you see the sign *Vendita Diretta* outside a vineyard, you may taste and buy the local wines. A sign saying *Cantine Aperte* means that the cellars are also open to the public.

Without seeing these signs, you may decide to visit spontaneously and be disappointed. Some estates are small and do not have the staff for drop-in visitors.

WE RECOMMEND THAT YOU TELEPHONE AND MAKE AN APPOINTMENT; YOUR PATIENCE WILL BE REWARDED.

Try to get a map from the Chianti Classico Consortium, located in San Casciano in Val di Pesa. It shows all the major Chianti producers, both in and out of the consortium. They have an excellent web site.

Consorzio del Marchino Storico Chianti Classico
Via Scopeti, 155
S. Andrea in Percussina
50026 San Casciano Val di Pesa
Florence
055 822 8501
fax 055 822 8173
www.chianticlassico.com

Many vineyards charge a fee for tastings and guided tour, some may charge extra for food to accompany tasting.

Greve and Panzano jointly host Vino al Vino, a wine festival held on the third weekend of September. Festivities take place in both towns.

For information call the Greve Tourism office
055 854 6404

Florence region

Azienda Agricola Colognole

Via del Palagio 15
Colognole Rufina, Firenze
055 831 9870
10.00-12.00, 14.00-18.00 daily
closed Saturday
credit cards accepted
English spoken
(from Rufina, take SS67 direction
Dicomano, take Colognole
turning and follow signs)
Owner Gabriella Spalletti
Trivelli inherited this fortified
medieval tower and decided
to restore the vineyard. She is
a member of Donne del Vino,
Women of Wine, and works
with her sons to make small
quantities of wine and olive
oil.

Tenuta di Capezzana

www.capezzana.it
Via Capezzana 100 Seano
50040 Carmignano, Firenze
055 870 6005
08.30-12.30, 14.30-18.30
Monday-Friday
by appointment only
credit cards accepted
English spoken
direct sale
(from A11 take Prato Ovest exit
direction Seano, Carmignano and
follow signs)
Wine has been produced here
since Etruscan times, and was
the first Tuscan DOC to be
allowed to use the 'French
Grape' Cabernet Sauvignon
in their Carmignano Rosso
DOCG. It was Caterina
Medici who first planted the
Cabernet vines at the villa
which was her residence.

Gaiole in Chianti

Castello di Brolio

www.ricasoli.it
Brolio 53013
0577 7301
08.00-12.00, 13.00-19.00 daily
11.00-19.00 Weekends
guided tastings by appointment
credit cards accepted
English spoken
This is the castle where
Chianti was invented, it has
been in the Ricasoli family
since the 12th century. They
produce two lines of wines:
quality *Castello di Brolio,* and
the more reasonably priced
Barone Ricasoli.

Badia a Coltibuono

www.coltibuono.com
closed November-February
vineyard:
0577 749 498
by appointment only
restaurant:
0577 749 424
lunch and dinner
closed Monday
booking advisable
shop:
0577 749 479
09.30-13.00, 14.00-19.00
closed Sunday
credit cards accepted
English spoken

(SS408 direction Chiantigiana 5km north of Gaiole in Chianti) Lorenza de Medici Stucchi makes her home in this restored abbey. There is a vineyard, restaurant, cooking school and shop selling both wine and farm produce.

Greve in Chianti

Le Cantine di Greve in Chianti

Piazza delle Cantine
055 854 6404
10.00-19.00 daily
The biggest selection of wines in Chianti, extra virgin olive oil, vin santo, and other locally produced goods.

Castello di Verrazzano

www.verrazzano.com
055 854 243
guided tour 11.00
Monday-Friday or by appointment
closed December, January
credit cards accepted
English spoken
(A1 to exit Firenze Sud
take SS222 to Greve
turn right after the sign for Greti)
Agritourismo rooms and suites available.
The castle is set in beautiful gardens which are included in the guided tour. All products from the farm can be tasted, including wild boar, and there is a range of tours available for booking.

Radda in Chianti

Podere Capaccia

www.poderecapaccia.com
Capaccia 53017
0577 738 385
09.00-12.00, 14.00-17.00
09.00-13.00, 14.00-19.00 Sunday
tastings by appointment
credit cards accepted
English spoken
direct sale
(From Radda, direction Castello d'Albola, take Montevertine turning. After 1km turn left.)
Giampaolo Pacini is an excellent host who enjoys promoting wine tourism. A visit here requires driving up a steep hill on a pot-holed white road, but once here, you will enjoy an excellent Chianti Classico which is often served with tasty nibbles. Giampaolo and his wife run Tuscan food seminars and sell olive oil and homemade products in addition to their rich red wines.

Montalcino

Brunello di Montalcino is made from just one grape, the Sangiovese. The fruit colours the wine a deep purple and gives it a rich, buttery taste. DOCG approved Brunello has matured two years in wood and two in the bottle for a minimum aging of four years. Riserva is aged an additional year. Rosso di Montalcino is matured only for one year.

The Brunello Consortium in the town centre has maps of the region showing all the producers. Many estates will allow a visit on fairly short notice if you ring in advance to book.

Consorzio del Vino Brunello di Montalcino

www.consorziobrunellodimont alcino.it
Costa del Municipio 1
0577 848 246
08.30-13.00, 15.00-18.00
Monday-Friday

Biondi-Santi

Il Greppo
0577 848 087
09.00-11.00, 15.00-17.00
Monday-Friday
tastings by appointment
closed weekends
credit cards accepted
English spoken
direct sale

The distinguished villa is approached along an avenue lined with cypresses. Franco Biondi-Santi is the fifth generation in the family credited with inventing Brunello. Some of their vintage wines are now collectors items.

Fattoria dei Barbi

www.fattoriadeibarbi.it
Fattoria dei Barbi e del Casato
0577 848 277
09.00-13.00, 15.00-18.00
Monday-Friday
14.30-17.30 Saturday-Sunday
tastings by appointment
credit cards accepted
English spoken
direct sale
Donatella Colombini Cinelli has transformed the cellars into an educational experience with paintings, videos, soil samples and other interesting information on the wine-making process. The family traces its origins back to the 13th century and many of the more colourful characters are represented. Fattoria dei Barbi also produces pecorino cheeses and farm-raised pork salami.

Montepulciano

Vino Nobile di Montepulciano is a red wine made from at least 80% Prugnolo Gentile grape. According to DOCG rules: Vino Nobile must be aged in wood for two years; the Reserva, for three years. Rosso di Montepulciano is also made from the Prugnolo Gentile grape but is not matured as long as Vino Nobile.

The Vino Nobile consortium has its headquarters in Montepulciano. Visitors can taste producers' wines in the on-site wine bar and can purchase wines from the shop.

Consorzio del Vino Nobile di Montepulciano

Palazzo del Capitano
Piazza Grande
53045 Montepulciano, Siena
0578 757 812
www.vinonobiledimontepulcia
no.it

Avignonesi

www.avignonesi.it
Via di Gracciano nel Corso 91
0578 724 304
09.30-13.30, 14.30-19.30 daily
by prior appointment only
closed December-February
credit cards accepted
English spoken
direct sale
The three Falvo brothers have created the perfect Tuscan wine estate: the beautiful country villa is approached along an avenue of cypress trees and is surrounded by vineyards. The wine is good too: Vino Nobile, Reservas, Super-Tuscan Desiderio, and a fresh Chardonnay are on sale here as well as in the 16th century palazzo in Montepulciano.

Valdipiatta

www.valipiatta.it
Via della Ciarliana 25/A
09.00-18.00 by appointment
closed weekends
credit cards accepted
English spoken
direct sale
(From Montepulciano take direction autostrada for 3.7km, turn right at the Valdipiatta sign.) The aging cantina has been hewed out of the hillside and tasting room is inside the mountain. The young owners are determined to make quality wines as ecologically as possible. Their Rosso di Montepulciano has more flavour than most and the white Il Nibbiano is light and refreshing on a hot day.

Lucca

Fattoria del Buonamico
Via Provinciale di Montecarlo 43
0583 220 38
08.30-12.30, 14.00-19.00
Monday-Friday
08.30-12.30 Saturday
closed Sunday
credit cards accepted
English spoken
direct sale
(from Montecarlo take direction
Altopascio for 1 km.
Fattoria is on the left)
One of the few Tuscan
vineyards to specialise in
white wine, the Montecarlo
Bianco DOC is a blend
of 50% Trebbiano, with
Pinot and Sauvignon. The
region's reputation for white
wine stretches back to the
Renaissance. A new addition
is Oro di Re, meaning 'the
king's gold', is a sweet wine
that goes well with pate and
cheese.

Azienda Agricola San Gervasio
www.sangervasio.com
San Gervasio di Palaia, Pontedera
0587 483 360
tastings 17.00-18.00 Wednesday
Or by appointment
08.00-12.00, 14.00-20.00
closed Sunday
credit cards accepted
English spoken
direct sale
(From Forcoli, take direction San
Gervasio, turn left at T junction

at top of hill for 1.3km)
Set in a castle that was once
home to the bishops of Lucca
and was the site of many
battles between Pisa and
Florence. San Gervasio is
an organic farm producing
white and red wines and it is
possible to order game birds,
wild boar and hare from the
large hunting reserve. There
is a museum of old farm tools
on the site.

Siena

Castello di Modanella
www.modanella.com
Modanella, Serre di Rapolano
0577 704 604, 704 553
08.30-13.00, 14.30-19.00
Monday-Friday
tastings by appointment only
credit cards accepted
English spoken
direct sale
(from the SS326, take direction
Modanella)
Located south-east of Siena
and set in a gothic 12th
century castle, this vineyard
produces single-variety
wines from grapes such as
Cabernet, Sangiovese, Merlot
and Canaiolo. The farm also
sells olive oil, Vin Santo and
organic produce.

SHOPPING

A SHOP IN SIENA

Florence

Duomo

Erborista Inglese
skin care
Via Tornabuorni 19
10.30-20.00 Tuesday-Saturday
15.30-20.00 Monday
closed two weeks in August
credit cards accepted
map C2
Persian Rose organic toners,
Diptych fragrances, all under
a frescoed ceiling in this
lovely shop that will leave
your skin glowing.

La Bottega dell'Olio
Piazza del Limbo 2r
055 267 0468
10.00-14.00, 15.00-20.00
Monday-Saturday
closed two weeks in January
credit cards accepted
map E2
All things made from the
olive and the olive tree.

Speziera Erborista
perfume
Palazzo Vecchio
Via Vaccherccia 9r
09.30-19.30 Monday- Saturday
open first and last Sunday of the
month
credit cards accepted
map e3
Beautiful apothecary, with
frescoed walls, makes
perfume and floral eau de
toilette whose combination of
scents fill the shop.

Oltrano

Arredamenti Castorina
home accessories
Via di Santo Sprito 13/15r
055 212 885
09.00-13.00, 15.30-19.30
Monday-Friday
09.00-13.00 Saturday
closed August
credit cards accepted
map B4
This family has been artisans
of wood objects since
1895. The shop is full of
architectural objects as well as
gilded music stands, cherubs,
obelisks, and other one-of-a-
kind items.

Giulio Giannini e Figlio
handmade marbled paper
Piazza Pitti 36r
055 212 621
10.00-19.30 Monday-Saturday
credit cards accepted
map C5
Large selection of marbled
books, some leather bound
with desk accessories to
match.

Il Torchio
handmade books
Via dei Bardi 17
055 234 2862
09.00-19.30 Monday-Friday
09.00-13.00 Saturday
closed Sunday
closed two weeks in August
credit cards accepted
map D4
Here you can watch the paper

marbling and book-binding. Stock up on beautifully unique journals, notebooks, albums and stationery.

Via Toscana
Piazza N Sauro 16r
055 219 948
10.00-13.00, 15.30-19.30
Tuesday-Saturday
15.30-19.30 Monday
closed August
credit cards accepted
map C4
Tuscan handicrafts, unbleached cotton robes, ceramics.

Santa Croce

Cartoleria Ecologica La Tartaruga
stationery
Borgo Albizi 60r
055 234 0845
09.30-19.30 Tuesday-Saturday
13.30-19.30 Monday
closed Sunday
credit cards accepted
map E4
Handmade paper and interesting stationery made out of recycled paper.

Leather School
leather bags and clothing
Piazza Santa Croce
Santa Croce church
map F4
Beautifully made leather goods, everything from custom tailored coats and jackets to bags, wallets and key fobs.

San Lorenzo

Giraffa
unusual items and gifts
Via Ginori, 20r
055 283 652
10.00-13.00, 15.30-19.30
Tuesday-Saturday
15.30-19.30 Monday
closed three weeks in August
credit cards accepted
map D1
Eastern and African lamps, Japanese ceramics, candles and other items.

Santa Maria Novella

Beltrami
shoes in small sizes
Via Panzani 1r
055 212 661
credit cards accepted
map C2
Shop carries assortment of shoes in sizes 34 and 35.

Farmacia di Santa Maria Novella
pharmacy
Via della Scala 16
055 216 276
09.00-19.30 Monday-Saturday
10.30-18.30 Sunday
closed two weeks in August
credit cards accepted
map C2
Antique pharmacy and herbalist set in a chapel complete with frescoes. The Aqua di Santa Maria Novella is considered to have a soothing effect.

SS = superstrada

The Mall
designer discount
Via Europa 8
Leccio, Reggello
0558 657 775
10.00-19.00 daily
15.00-19.00 Sunday
closed Tuesday afternoons
La Perla, Ungaro, Valentino, Gucci, Ferragamo, Saint Laurent, Sergio Rossi discounted 60 per cent and more. From the A1 Autostrada take the exit marked Incisa. Stay on your right towards Pontassieve until you reach Leccio. The Mall is just the other side of the town centre.
There is a shuttle bus service from Florence to and from The Mall. Telephone for booking and information.

Dolce & Gabbana
designer discount
S. Maria Maddalena
Pian dell'Isola 49
055 833 1300
09.00-19.00 Monday-Saturday
Excellent deals in menswear, ladies clothing and handbags.

Arezzo

I Pellettieri d'Italia
designer discount
Localita Levanella 69
0978 9188
09.30-13.00, 14.00-18.30
Prada and Miu Miu discount mall, often busy with Japanese coach tours.

Colle di Val D'Elsa

Arnolfo di Cambio
crystal
Pian dell'Olmino 53034
SS 541, 8 kms south of Colle
0577 928 279
09.00-12.30, 15.30-19.00 daily
closed Sunday
credit cards accepted
English spoken
In a town known for crystal, this studio factory is at the cutting edge of design and is worth a visit to view Arnolfo's creations. The Bacco line of wine glasses is designed to bring out the flavours of a particular wine and features a special glass for Brunello. The company also produces china by top Italian designers such as Roberto Cavalli, and seconds are sometimes available in the factory shop at reduced prices.

Gaiole in Chianti

Bianchi self-service
Via Ricasoli 48
0577 749 501
08.00-20.00 daily
English spoken
A friendly grocery store that sells good home-baked bread and ingredients for a picnic or an easy dinner at the villa. There are tables out front for light meals and snacks.

Greve in Chianti

Antica Macelleria-Norcineria Falorni
cheese shop and butcher
Piazza Matteotti 69/71
055 853 029
08.00-13.00, 15.30-19.30 daily
credit cards accepted
English spoken
A stuffed wild boar stands outside Falorni's shop under the arches of Greve's main square. The shop stocks local Chianina beef and pork products and classic salame Toscano. A large selection of local pecorino cheeses are stored in the cellar.

THE CHEESE CELLAR

Montecatini Terme

Montecatini is known for two kinds of biscuits: *brigidini*, light-as-air crispy wafers flavoured with anise and *cialde,* a brittle golden medallion of crushed almonds between two wafers.

Pasticceria Bargilli
biscuit
Viale Grocco 2
0572 794 59
08.00-13.00, 15.30-20.00
closed winter Mondays
closed January
no credit cards
The Bargilli family has been making *le cialde* since 1936 and they are fast becoming the town's most popular souvenir.

Pasticceria Desideri
biscuits
Via Gorizia 5
Piazzeta Bicchierai
0572 710 88
08.30-13.00, 16.00-20.00
closed winter Mondays
closed February
no credit cards

The Desideri family has been making *brigidini* since before 1900 and has been winning cookery prizes for them since 1918. Once made by hand, the biscuits are now made on a top-secret machine designed by the family.

Montepulciano

Formaggi Silvana Cugusi
cheese
Via della Boccia 8
SS 146 per Pienza
3 kms outside Montepulciano
0578 757 558
08.00-13.00, 15.00-19.30 daily
no credit cards

The Cugusi family make the finest sheep's cheeses in Tuscany using old recipes brought from Sardinia 50 years ago. The ricotta is creamy and delicate, hand stirred by Giovanna. Here is where you can purchase the real *pecorini di Pienza* in different stages of maturation, all hand turned.

Il Frantoio
olive oil
Via di Martiena 2
0578 758 732 shop
0578 716 305 mill
10.00-13.00, 16.00-19.30
closed Wednesday afternoons
and summer Sundays
credit cards accepted

The frantoio sells several grades of oil, the best has a subtle flavour of cut grass, with a peppery finish, that is the characteristic of Tuscan olive oil. In winter, oil is sold from the mill.

Avignonesi
wine
Via di Gracciano nel Corso 91
0578 724 304
09.30-13.30, 14.30-19.30 daily
closed December–February
credit cards accepted
English spoken

An elegant 16th century palazzo houses the shop for the wine estate belonging to three brothers of the Falvo family who have merged lands. They have imbued the estate with their passion for wine and offer a Vino Nobile and its Riservas, a rich Merlot/Cabernet blend and a light Chardonnay. Avignonesi also sells olive oil.

Enoteca Oinochoe

wine
Via di Voltaia nel Corso 82
0578 757 524
09.00-19.00 daily
closed Sunday
closed January-February
credit cards accepted

Chiara Bellacci stocks all the
Nobile and Brunello wines
from the surrounding region
as well as Chianti and a good
variety of super-Tuscans.
A good place to stock up.

Pienza

La Cornucopia Club delle Fattorie

specialty foods
Piazza Martiri della Liberta 2
0578 748 150
09.30-13.00, 14.30-19.30
closed Tuesday
closed Wednesday mornings in
winter
credit cards accepted
English spoken

Alberto and Mara del Buono
are champions of artisan food
and never sell anything they
don't like to eat or drink. The
shop is filled with sauces and
pastas, special vinegars and
olive oil, biscuits and cheese.
A perfect place to come and
pick up a meal to prepare and
enjoy at your accommodation.

Ceramica della Mezzaluna

ceramics
Via Gozzante 67
0578 748 561
09.00-13.00, 15.00-18.00
closed Sunday

Dino and Fabrizio specialise
in ceramic tiles and objects
with bright colours and
unusual shapes. Their shop
has a great view of the Val
d'Orcia.

Pisa

Coltelleria Fontana

knives
Corso Italia 124
050 413 69
map D4

Knives are a must-have tool
for any chef and this shop has
an extensive range, including
ravioli cutters, pasta wheels,
nut crackers and other items
not readily found in the UK.

Melani

kitchenware
Corso Italia 44
050 502 323
map E4

A large shop stocking
pots and pans, decorative
glassware, Alessi cooking
ware and fine decanters from
Villeroy and Bremer.

De Bondt
chocolate
Via Turati 22
Corte San Domenico
050 501 896
10.00-13.00, 16.00-20.00
closed Monday
closed Sunday afternoon
English spoken
credit cards accepted
map D5

Hand-dipped chocolates made by the Dutch owner, Paul de Bondt. His Italian wife, Cecilia Cacobelli designs the packaging and the shop's clean, modern interior. The ganache-filled chocolates are light and creamy with finely balanced flavours.

L'Altra Roba
Organic food
Piazza delle Vettovaglie 3
050 598 987
08.00-13.00, 16.00-20.00
closed Wednesday afternoon
closed Sunday
English spoken
no credit cards
map E3

Pisa's central food market is just north of the river, off the Via Vigna. The porticoed square contains a temporary food market in the centre with permanent shops around the edge. L'Altra Roba stocks every pulse and grain found in Italy as well as organic products, whether fresh, preserved or frozen. Be sure to pick up a loaf of the fabulous organic bread.

Pistoia

Confetteria Corsini
confetti
Piazza San Francesco D'Assisi 43
0573 201 38
08.00-13.00, 16.00-19.00
closed Sunday and summer
Saturday afternoons
closed two weeks in August
no credit cards
English spoken

Confetti, hard white candies with a core of almond or chocolate, are a traditional Italian candy wrapped in tulle and given away at joyful family occasions. This shop, owned by the Corsini family, was commissioned to make 16th century blue confetti for the film *Casanova* and still retains the old machinery.

Radda in Chianti

Ceramiche Rampini
ceramics
Casa Beretone di Vistarenni
From Radda, take the Gaiole road for 2 km
0577 738 043
09.00-18.00
closed Sunday
credit cards accepted
English spoken

Guiseppe Rampini continues a Renaissance tradition with dinner services made specially for ceremonial events. The Medici had different plates designed for each season. The Rampini family have simplified these designs for their line of colourful ceramics, made from clay found along the Arno river.

Castello di Volpaia
vinegar, olive oil, wine
Piazza Cisterna1, Volpaia
From Radda, take the Greve road for 4 kms
0577 738 066
09.00-20.00 daily
closed February
credit cards accepted
English spoken
The real treat here is the selection of superb vinegars made from wine using the ancient methods. Wine is infused with oxygen and aerated slowly for 20 days to make vinegar, which is then aged in oak barrels The vinegars are flavoured with herbs, flowers and spices.

San Gimignano

Bottega D'Arte Povera
crafts
Via San Matteo 83
0577 941 951
10.00-19.00 daily
closed Monday in winter
credit cards accepted
Arte povera means poor art, or things that are handmade from the land, terra-cotta cooking pots, chestnut baskets, teardrop baskets and olive wood bowls and salad forks that survive for years.

La Buca di Montauto
wild boar
Via San Giovanni 16
0577 940 407
08.30-21.00 in summer
10.00-19.00 in winter
closed Tuesday in winter
credit cards accepted
English spoken
Wild boar has a stronger flavour than pork, more peppery with a dense texture. Signora Capezzuoli's shop sells sausages, hams, salami and locally produced saffron. Try the al tartufo salame which is made with truffles.

Teruzzi & Puthod
wine
Ponte a Rondolino Casale 19
Just outside San Gimignano
0577 940 143
08.00-12.00, 14.00-18.00
closed Saturday and Sunday
credit cards accepted
English spoken
Ex-jockey Enrico Teruzzi and his French ballerina wife, Carmen Puthod, have established the white wine Vernaccia di San Gimignano as one of the best in Italy. The shop only sells its wine in cases of a dozen or more.

Siena

Antica Drogheria Manganelli 1879

specialty foods
Via di Citta 71/73
0577 280 002
summer
09.00-20.00 daily
winter
09.00-13.00, 15.30-19.30
closed Wednesday afternoon
credit cards accepted
English spoken
map D3

Antique cabinets are stacked to the ceiling with gourmet items of all description. Everything from designer olives to truffles, jams and a whole room devoted to wines and grappas. The traditional Sienese pastries are made from centuries old recipes passed down through the Manganelli family.

Consorzio Agrario Siena

supermarket
Via Pianigiani 9
0577 2301
summer
07.45-13.00, 17.00-20.00
closed Saturday afternoon
winter
07.45-13.00, 16.30-19.30
closed Sunday and Wednesday afternoon
credit cards accepted
map D2

A supermarket run by a farmers consortium and featuring foods from the province of Siena. Under the brand name Granducato, members sell their locally produced olive oil and wine at reasonable prices. The shop also stocks cheese, salami, grain, honey and other local foods and has branches in Montalcino, Pienza, Buonconvento and Chianciano Terme.

Enoteca Italiana

wine store and bar
Fortezza Medicea
0577 288 497
12.00-01.00 Tuesday-Saturday
12.00-20.00 Monday
closed Sunday
credit cards accepted
English spoken
map A1

Italy's state-run wine cellar is suitably located in a grand old Medici fortress. Over 800 varieties of wines are offered for sale and there are professional tasters to assist in making your purchase. Upstairs is a wine bar where the wines may be bought by the glass for modest prices. Enoteca Italiana also organises guided wine tastings, concerts and a Wine Week held annually in June.

Lorenza de Medici Shop
ceramics and gifts
Via di Citta 47
0577 477 55
09.00-19.00
credit cards accepted
map D3

This is the new shop owned by the heiress to the grand Medici name, which no longer carries the power it once did. However, Lorenza has inherited a good eye for tasteful objects and has gathered them together in her shop just off the Campo. Palio coffee cups decorated with the emblems of the 17 contrade make a lovely gift or souvenir.

Forno dei Galli-Sclavi
bread
Via dei Termini 45
07.30-13.15, 17.00-19.30
closed Saturday afternoon
closed Sunday
map D2

Siena has a reputation for specialty baking and this is the historic bakery. The pane basso is very good, crisp on the outside and soft on the inside. Another Sienese bread is the schiacciate which is a flat yeast bread dotted with raisins or olives. Or try the flat, crumbly ciaccina friabile. Sclavi has many outlets in Siena and all of them sell a variety of Sienese bread, pastry and cakes.

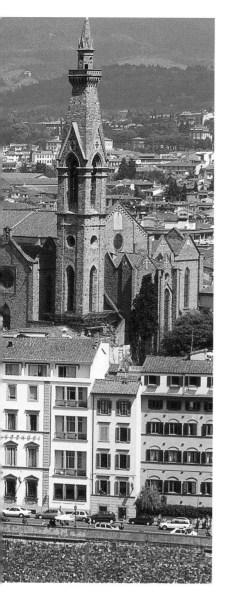

TRAVEL BASICS

Baggage

Keep baggage to a minimum, bearing in mind that narrow streets and traffic restrictions can make it impossible for vehicles to reach your hotel. If you are staying in a villa, you may have to negotiate steps, a slope or a pathway. Pack light, you can always purchase what you need in Italy.

Cabin baggage should fit into the overheads and regulations state that it must not be larger than 45 cm x 32 cm x 22 cm or over 5 kilos in weight.

Airlines are searching hand baggage and confiscating sharp objects including: manicure scissors, shaving razors, cutlery, Swiss army knives etc. These items should be packed into checked luggage.

Medication should travel in your hand luggage. If you are under treatment carry a doctor's letter detailing your condition. A carry cot or fully collapsible wheelchair will normally be stored in the cargo hold. Contact the airline in advance to make arrangements. There is a non smoking policy on all airlines.

- Don't leave bags unattended
- Pack your own luggage
- Never carry items onto an aircraft for someone else
- Cameras and film should be taken as hand luggage
- Check-in staff will ask you about your baggage; it is a criminal offence to give false information

Cash points

Bank machines in Italy are plentiful and easy to use. Transactions can be made in English. Amounts can be withdrawn as needed from your account, which is better for personal security. Bank charges per transaction vary between £1 and £2.

Italian airports have cash points in their terminals so it is possible to wait until arrival to withdraw holiday cash. Carry a few euro coins for carts or coffee. Machine withdrawals are quicker than cashing traveller's cheques at a bank and may offer a better exchange rate.

Credit card purchases may net a better rate of exchange than cash point withdrawals from your bank account. However, many transactions in Italy are paid in cash only.

Documents

- Passport Agency
  0870 521 0410
  www.passport.gov.uk
- Italian Consulate
  0208 235 9371

- Foreign,Commonwealth office
  www.knowbeforeyougo.co.uk

Passports should be valid six months after travelling. A visa is not necessary for British and EC passport holders. Non-EC citizens should check with their own or with the Italian Consulate.

Telephones

To access mailbox and answering services you need to set up a PIN before you depart. Calls made to your mobile are charged at the local rate to the caller. However you will be charged for receiving the call whilst abroad. Screening calls can save considerable expense, as can text messaging.

To call UK mobiles from abroad, dial 0044 and mobile number but drop the zero at the front of the number.

To call Italy from abroad, dial 0039 then the number including the area prefix. Within Italy dial the full number including the zero.

After check-in

Proceed through to the departure lounge until the departure gate is displayed on the monitors. Gates are usually assigned a short time before departure so it is a good idea to make your way to the gate as soon as the number is assigned. Sometimes it is a long walk and late arrivals at the gate may be denied boarding the aircraft.

Flight delays

If there is a delay and you have taken travel insurance, you may be eligible for compensation. To make a claim contact:
Claims International Limited
South London House
297 High Street
Croydon
CR0 1QH

020 8680 5141

The claim must be backed by a letter confirming the delay, which should be obtained directly from the airline.

Eurotunnel

Plan to arrive well in advance of the time stated on your tickets. Remember to carry your Vehicle Registration Book (logbook) with you. This must be either in your name as the owner of the vehicle, or you must have written consent from the owner to drive the car. It is important to note that no LPG (gas powered) vehicles are allowed on Eurotunnel trains.

Pisa Airport
www.pisa-airport.com

•Information
 050 500 707
•Lost and Found
 050 849 400

Pisa is a small airport with one terminal, housing arrivals and departures at opposite ends of the building.

Cash points are located between arrivals and departures. On exiting the baggage reclaim area, the car hire desks are straight ahead. Pisa can become very busy during high season, especially on Saturdays. Queues for car hire can be very long, we suggest one of your party goes ahead to the desk while the others wait for luggage. To save time, you may also be able to pre-register with your car hire company over the internet.

Train tickets to Florence may be obtained from the ticket office to the right of the arrivals area. It is advisable to purchase tickets for the return journey as the ticket queues at the Florence train station can be very long and slow moving.

Trains to Florence

Direct trains to Florence leave from the platform adjacent to the departures area of the airport building, to the left of arrivals. The service operates from 10.18, then hourly from 12.33 to 18.50. On Sundays, it operates until 16.33, after which there is a train at 19.09. The journey takes one hour on the express train or 90 minutes on the slow train.

The coach service to Florence departs Pisa airport at 11.30, 15.00 and 22.20 and takes 90 minutes.

The train to Florence and Pisa city depart from the far end of the departures hall. At the time of printing the taxi fare to Florence was around €100.

If you are arriving on a late flight and are staying in secluded property, book into a hotel and continue your journey afresh in the morning. Many villas are set in the Tuscan countryside and are reached via roads which are largely unmade and not well lit in night time.

Santa Maria Novella station

Located in the centre of the Florence. Taxis are available outside the station and the fare to most tour operator hotels is around €10.

Florence Airport

- Information desk
  055 315 874
- Flight information
  055 306 1300

Cash points and the car hire desk are located in the arrivals terminal.

A car is not recommended in Florence because of traffic restrictions and a shortage of parking spaces. Drivers may be asked to produce confirmation of hotel occupancy. Traffic restrictions and narrow streets in the historic centre make access difficult to the following hotels:
Brunelleschi, Monna Lisa, Botticelli, Gallery Art, Helvetia & Bristol, Porta Rossa.
Few hotels have their own car parks but the reception desk will usually know the nearest private car park. It is common to be charged €20 per day.

Bus number 62 runs to the city centre from Florence airport every 25 minutes and costs €4 . The 25 minute taxi journey costs around €20.

Train Travel

Long distance and fast services require prior reservation. Stamp your tickets at the yellow boxes situated by the entrance to the platform before boarding the train.

- *EC, Eurocity*
  fast international train
- *IC, Intercity*
  fast national train
- *Espresso*
  long-distance fast train
- *Diretto*
  long-distance stops at main stations
- *Regionale*
  local stopping train

Passengers who fail to validate their tickets may be fined €10.

Bus Travel

Purchase tickets in advance of travel from newstands, tabachi or bars. Most city buses operate on a flat fare system, however long the journey. Ask about special passes for tourists or day travel.

Validate the ticket in the stamping machine on the bus. The front and rear doors are usually for boarding the bus and the middle is usually the exit.

Car Hire

Documentation

- Passport
- Car hire voucher
- Current UK driving licence
- Credit card

The UK driving licence, valid for at least one year prior to travel, must have both parts and be translated into Italian. If your licence was issued in another country, you will need to check with the car company to see if you require any other documentation.

The credit card is a guarantee and must be the same name as the hirer of the vehicle. Cash deposits are not accepted. You will be asked to sign the conditions of hire. This is the contract between you and the rental company. It is wise to keep a copy of this agreement after your return home in case of any subsequent queries.

Optional Insurances

The optional waiver to cover the CDW excess and to cover the TP excess are a source of commissionable sales revenue for the local car hire office. Charges for these are payable locally and will be added to your credit card. Initial and sign the car hire rental agreement in two places to accept the conditions of these two coverages. Do not initial the rental agreement for any additional insurances (ie Super CDW, Super TP, PAI, Super PAI) that you do not require.

Check the spare tyre before embarking on a journey. If this is stolen a police report must be obtained otherwise the cost of the replacement will be charged by the car hire company.

Road fund licence fee

This *Registration Fee* is a local tax and will be charged to your credit card at a rate of €2 per day, plus tax, to a maximum charge of six days.

Rules of the road

Italians drive on the right-side of the road. Check both ways before crossing roads, especially during the first couple of days after you arrive. Be aware of the local regulations. These are available from your local car hire company.

Italians like to drive fast and have little patience for the struggling tourist. They will honk, flash their headlights and drive around a vehicle who hesitates. Ignore them, focus on the road, and enjoy driving in Italy.

You must carry your current driving licence at all times, with an Italian translation, and another form of identification, preferably with photograph.

Drinking and driving laws are similar to the UK and penalties include on-the-spot fines or, as in the UK, imprisonment for more serious offences.

Seat belts are compulsory and children should travel in rear seats.

The minimum age for driving in Italy is 18 but car hire companies also have their own restrictions.

Dipped headlights should be used in tunnels.

An interior mirror and left-hand side mirror are compulsory.

Sound your horn to give warning of your approach on tiny mountain roads.

The motorway

Italy's motorways are well provided with petrol stations, cafes and restaurants, and the distance between them is clearly signposted.

Italians drive on the right-hand side of the road. This means that roundabouts, through lanes, and on and off ramps are located opposite to what British drivers encounter.

Right of way belongs to main roads only if marked with a yellow diamond on a white background. In all other cases give way to traffic coming from the right. This also applies when you're on a roundabout.

When entering a motorway care is needed in following signs and at entrances/exits. Don't be afraid to approach at a lower speed.

Motorway signs are always green and tolls are normally charged. Do not use the lanes reserved for Telepass cardholders unless there is no alternative.

Collect your ticket by pressing the red button at the automatic booth and proceed onto the motorway.

At the exit, hand in your ticket and pay the toll, which will be displayed on an illuminated panel. Short stretches of motorway may display a fixed charge at the entry toll. To pay by credit card use the channels marked ViaCARD.

Speed limits

- motorways, depending on motor size
  110 km, up to 1099cc
  130 km, over 1099cc

- open roads 90 km

- built up areas 50 km

- blue zone in cities 30 km

Fines for speeding are heavy and are payable on the spot or at the local police station (Vigili Urbani). The police must give you a receipt for the amount of the fine paid. Alternatively, fines may be debited to your credit card, having already been forwarded to the car hire company.

Signs

- *Strada dissetata/Strada deformata*
  rough or gravel road

- *Senso Unico*
  one way.

- *a yellow diamond on a white background*
  right of way

- *white P on a blue background*
  designated parking area

- *Zona Disco*
  pay and display

- Yellow lines
  parking prohibited

Security

- Always leave windows closed and doors locked

- Never leave any valuables in the car

- If it is absolutely necessary

to leave belongings in the car, lock them in the boot

- Park in guarded car parks

- Beware of other drivers who 'flash' you to stop

In the event of car theft, the local car hire agency and the police must be informed immediately.

Breakdowns

If you break down, dial 116 at the nearest phone and tell the operator where you are, the type of car and your registration number; the Italian Automobile Club (ACI) will send someone to fix your car. This not a free service but is cheaper than joining the ACI outright.

Accidents

In the event of an accident involving other vehicles, or pedestrians, it is of vital importance that the CID form, supplied in car documents, is filled out with full details of all vehicles involved, ie number plate and model of car. Both parties need to sign the CID form. Do not move the car until the police arrive.

Arriving at your Villa

Drive directly to your villa as there may be someone on site waiting to welcome you. Villa owners may travel some distance to be on the premises when you arrive. Some villas are reached by unmade roads or dirt tracks, perhaps without lighting, so take extra care if arriving after dark.

An inventory of equipment in your villa or apartment is normally provided and should be checked against the contents. Report any missing or damaged items to prevent you being charged for the cost of replacements.

Villas are cleaned for your arrival which is usually 16.00. If time is short between the departure and arrival of guests, a little wait may be unavoidable. Linen will be usually be changed once a week and may be left on beds for your arrival or for changeover.

Swimming pools will only be open from June-September. Small hand towels may be provided but larger bath and beach towels are not normally included.

Villa owners will have left information on the operation of the gas/electricity and utilities; how and where to dispose of rubbish, what to do if you have a maintenance problem and contact details.

Voltage is 220 and adaptors can be bought in the UK for Italian 2-pin points.

Kitchen equipment varies with each property and is usually less comprehensive than in a permanent home. It may not include teapots, kettles, toasters and egg-cups, as these are rarely used in the Italian household. A draining rack, placed in a cupboard over the sink, is commonly found in Italian kitchens where 'drying up' is not the usual practice.

Televisions may not always receive English channels. Irons are rarely supplied and often holiday homes are equipped with un-matching furniture and fittings .

Cots are supplied when requested at the time of booking and charges are payable on arrival.
Most foods and basics cost less than at home, and eating in restaurants is generally cheaper, as are local wines and spirits.

In a warm climate it is important to put food away and tie rubbish in a plastic bag before placing in the dustbins to avoid attracting animals.

If your accommodation has a gas cooker, always double check that it has been turned off properly, just as you would at home, and follow any gas safety instructions. In many cases you will find that the gas is supplied direct from a bottle – as an extra precaution, turn the supply off at the bottleneck when it is not in use.

Some properties may not provide a shower mat. As floors are often tiled and you will be using a bath or shower which is unfamiliar to you, be careful to ensure that you do not slip.

Although it seems obvious, you should never allow strangers into your villa. Thieves posing as cleaners have been known to carry out burglaries while guests are still in the villa.

On departure, vacate the villa by 10.00 Be sure to take all your belongings.

Agriturismo

Increasingly popular are holidays on an Italian farm. The emphasis is on an informal atmosphere to experience traditional Italy in the relaxing countryside.

Meals are often prepared from the freshly grown ingredients and the wine is usually homemade.

Many properties have been restored and swimming pools installed, while retaining the original beauty and charm.

Animals

The hygiene and care of animals overseas differs vastly from the UK. It is advisable not to feed or play with animals, either wild or domestic. If bitten or scratched by an animal, seek medical assistance.

Hotels

Hoteliers will try to ensure that your room is ready for occupation on your arrival, but if you arrive on an early flight be prepared for a possible wait until lunchtime.

In some hotels, especially older or listed properties, you may find that there is a variation in the size and shape of rooms on offer. Single rooms will usually be a room with one single bed instead of a double for sole occupancy. Televisions may only receive Italian channels or a limited amount of English channels.

Fire safety

For your own safety, make sure you know the location of the fire exit nearest to your room/apartment and read carefully all fire safety information.

Meals

Evening meals are taken at a later time in Italy. At some hotels it is possible to request an earlier sitting. Don't be surprised if you are given a dinner menu during breakfast for you to pre-select your evening meal: some hotel prefer to obtain fresh produce on a daily basis and will purchase only the ingredients required for one meal. At the beginning or end of the season, some facilities in your accommodation may not be available.

Italian Bars

These are functional places, all very similar in decor: brightly lit, chrome counter, Gaggia coffee machine and pictures of local football heroes on the wall. It's cheaper to stand at the bar to drink so business is brisk as locals, usually men in rural areas, gather for a quick espresso and pastry in the morning or beer and panini lunch.

Most are not open late because after the evening *passegiata*, socialising tends to happen in restaurants.

In Italy it is usual to have water and a glass or two of wine with each meal, but it is not so usual to go out for a drink. You'll rarely see drunks in public and over-indulgence is frowned upon, especially in women.

Children of all ages are welcomed in restaurants and cafés where family parties are a normal part of Italian social life.

Museums & Churches

Usual opening hours are 09.00-13.00, 15.00-19.00. However, many are only open in the mornings. Most museums and galleries are closed on Mondays. If a visit to a particular site is planned, check ahead to make sure that there is not a holiday or fete affecting usual openings.

State museums are free to persons over 65 and under 18.

Remember the dress code when visiting churches and dress modestly. Arms and legs should be covered on both men and women.

Carry a small hand mirror to view painted ceilings.

Tabacconists

Cigarettes can only be purchased from licensed tobacconists identified by a white T on a black background (*Tabacchi*). These shops often close by 20.00.

Some bars will sell cigarettes after hours and there are vending machines tucked into doorways, but these often charge premium prices.

Tipping

Tipping is at your discretion but, as a guide, approximately €5 per week for hotel maids and €6 per person per week in the hotel restaurant is acceptable.

In restaurants a service charge is normally included, so anything extra is at your discretion.

Railway and airport porters charge a fixed tip of approximately €3-5 per piece of luggage. This is also the amount to tip a hotel porter.

Tip 10 per cent of the fare for taxi.

Toilets

Public toilets are rare in Italy so take advantage of toilets in bars and museums

Public telephones

Hotels in Italy usually apply an expensive surcharge to telephone calls. A telephone card (*scheda*), may be obtained from a Tabacchi. Remove the perforated corner before using. A red flashing light indicates that the telephone is out of order.

Directory enquiries:

- Italy, 12
- Europe, 176
- Rest of world, 170
- Country direct, 172
  dial 172 and then 0044 to speak to an operator in your own language.

Postage

Postage from Italy to the UK currently costs €0.41 for letters and postcards. Stamps may be bought at post offices or tobacconists.

Supermarkets

Poggibonsi

Co-op

does not accept credit cards.
08.00-21.00 Tuesday-Friday
08.00-20.30 Saturday
14.00-21.00 Monday
closed Sundays
From Florence take the second Poggibonsi exit off the Fi-Si (Firenze – Siena) superstrada heading in direction of Siena. From Siena take the first exit in the direction of Florence.

Superal

credit cards accepted
12.00-20.00 Monday
08.00-20.00 Tuesday-Saturday
8.00-13.00 summer Sundays
closed winter Sundays
Take the Poggibonsi north
exit off Fi-Si superstrada
(not autostrada). Follow the
signs for San Giminagno, the
Superal is at the roundabout.

Pisa

Co-op

does not accept credit cards.
08.00-21.00 Tuesday-Friday
08.00-20.30 Saturday
14.00-21.00 Monday
closed Sundays
A hypermarket COOP is
about ten minutes from Pisa
just off superstrada.

Health and Safety

Sunbathing

Always cover yourself with a
high factor sunscreen lotion
that offers good protection.
Never stay in the sun until
your skin goes red as the
damage will have already
been done. Take particular
care with children, who
should always use sunscreen
or cover up with a sun hat
and loose cotton clothing.

The sun's rays are at their
strongest between the hours
of 11.00 and 15.00 when you
can also burn in the shade,
when it's cloudy or when
you are swimming. Wind
and water intensify the sun's
effect so while you may feel
cool, you could be burning.

Drink plenty of water as this
will combat dehydration,
which is responsible for
the nausea and dizziness
associated with heat stroke.
Avoid alcohol because it will
dehydrate you further.

Alcohol

Do not drink before
swimming in the pool or
in the sea and try to avoid
drinking when sunbathing
as this will dehydrate you.
Never drink if hiring a car as
drink-driving laws are strict
in Italy

Medical treatment

The E111 form entitles UK
residents to free medical
treatment and to pay for
prescriptions at the local
rate. It is avaiable at UK post
offices.

Before seeking treatment, if
possible, the form should be
exchanged for a 'certificate
of entitlement' at the local
Unita Sanitaria Locale who
will supply a list of doctors
and dentists. If you need
emergency treatment, go
to the *pronto soccorso*, A&E,
department of the nearest
hospital.

Collect receipts for any treatment you receive and any medicine purchased.

It is important that you bring your insurance documents with you. This applies, even if you have insurance via your credit card company or as an extension of your house insurance. If you need treatment or emergency recovery, it is essential that you have the details of the medical assistance company and also your policy number. If you are hospitalised it is important that you inform the insurance company as soon as possible.

Doctors

The majority of hotels are connected to a local doctor who will visit your hotel on request. You will usually have to pay for this service and then reclaim on your insurance when you return home.

Dentists

The E111 form entitles citizens of EU countries to free dental treatment by going to the *Unita Sanitaria Locale* for a certificate.

Private dentist costs may be able to be reclaimed, depending on your policy.

Chemists

Most chemists will have a list of doctors and dentists.

Chemists are usually open 09.00-20.00, closing for lunch in rural areas. Many pharmacists speak English and can assist with minor ailments. In Italy, medicine is often given by suppository so be sure to ask the chemist.

The chemist will ask you to pay a percentage of the cost of each prescription medicine plus a fixed charge per item. Keep the receipts to support any claim you make.

Supermarkets carry aspirin, skin creams, plasters and various dressings for minor accidents.

Personal security

Keep your valuables, in particular your jewellery, in a safety deposit box or another secure place within your accommodation.

Be aware: charming barrios and shopping lanes are a magnet for pickpockets and purse snatchers. Try not to consult maps in open view and beware of strangers asking you directions. Do not walk alone at night in narrow dark areas. Keep to well lit, busy areas.

Carry your cash and your cards separately, and only carry the amount of cash that you need on a daily basis. Keep a three day supply of cash in your hotel safe to meet expenses in case your cards must be replaced.

Leave nothing of value in parked cars.

Credit card companies contact details

Lost or stolen credit card contact numbers are open 24 hours. Prefix 0044.

- Abbey National
  1908 344 900
- American Express
  1273 696 933
- Barclays Bank
  1604 230 230
- Clydesdale Bank
  1132 881 403
- Egg
  1268 298 807
- First Direct
  1132 345 678
- Giro Bank
  1519 441 220
- HSBC
  1442 422 929
- Lloyds TSB
  1702 278 270
- Nat West Bank
  1132 778 899
- Royal Bank of Scotland
  1268 298 929
- TSB Trustcard
  1273 204 471

Police report

Depending on the severity of the incident, you may decide it is not worth more precious holiday time spent at a police station. Stolen items are rarely recovered and most credit card companies are usually satisfied with a telephone report from the cardholder. However, if a large amount was stolen, and you will be making an insurance claim, a police report will be required.

Italian Police

In Italy there are many types of police:

- *Polizia Urbana*
  Traffic and parking police

- *Polizia Stradele*
  Patrol motorways

- *Police Statale*
  Thefts and petty crime

- *Carabinieri*
  Military police, general crime, public order, drug control. The real police.

Telephone numbers

- 113
  Police or ambulance

- 112
  Carabinieri

- 115
  Fire Brigade,
  Vigili del Fuoco

Departures

Pisa airport

Departures check-in is at the right of the building. Luggage trolleys are free.

The departure gates are to the left of the check-in area, almost opposite the bar. It is advisable to wait for your flight to be announced before entering as seating is less comfortable.

After passport and security, there is also a small bar although opening times are erratic and the bar is often closed. There are no shops.

Watch the monitors for updates. The Executive Lounge is on the first floor. Smoking is permitted in the bar.

Shops

There are several small shops selling clothes, souvenirs, and sunglasses. A small shop next to the arrivals area sells English newspapers, stamps and telephone cards. Cigarettes should be bought here.

Toilets

These are on the first floor and near the bar area on the ground floor, where there are also baby-changing facilities. First Aid facilities are next to left luggage and the car hire desks in the arrivals section.

Bars/restaurants

There is one bar, situated at the centre of the building, selling drinks, sandwiches, pizzas and confectionery. Pay and obtain a receipt at the cash desk before ordering at the counter.

During the summer there is an outside eating area which is usually open 06.30-22.00. A self-service restaurant is on the first floor, generally open 11.30-15.00 and 18.30-21.00. There is a separate area for waiter service but this is not always available.

Returning your car

Allow the following times for travel to Pisa airport in order to return your car and check in. This is in addition to the two hours before flight departure time.

- From North Tuscany allow at least two hours

- From South Tuscany (Siena/ Montepulciano/Montalcino) allow at least threehours

- From Central Tuscany (San Gimignano/Chianti/Casole) allow at least two hours

Do not use the time it took you to reach your holiday destination as a guideline for your return journey as the roads to Pisa and the coast may be subject to heavy traffic and delays. This is especially true on summer weekends when Italians head for the beach.

On arriving at Pisa airport follow the signs for car hire return. After parking please ensure that lights are switched off, all personal belongings have been removed, and all doors are locked and windows closed. The keys and documents must be returned either to a representative of the car hire company on site, or to the car hire desk, in order to close the contract.

Petrol stations

Stations near Pisa airport are:

- Q8, approximately 8 kms from the airport travelling on the superstrada from Florence. This is the most convenient place to fill up.

- For the airport petrol station, driving from Florence on the Fi-Pi-Li superstrada, take the second left (approx 50 m after first left) after you have exited the superstrada for Pisa airport. The first left also takes you to the airport but you will miss the petrol station.

- On Via Aeroporto, the main road from the airport to the centre of Pisa. May be closed on Sundays.

- Via Aurelia, the road from Pisa to Viareggio. Open 8.00-12.00, 15.00-19.00. Alternatively fill up at Q8 on the superstrada.

Florence airport

If you are returning a car, the Avis desk is situated in the Arrivals terminal.

A coffee bar on the first floor of the departure terminal sells a selection of sandwiches and snacks.

A self-service restaurant on the first floor of the arrivals terminal is open for lunch only. Flight monitors are displayed in the restaurant.

The commercial shopping area of the airport is open daily from 06.00–20.30. After passport control there are two duty free shops.

Index

A

Academy of Fine Arts 42
Accademia 18, 20, 42
Agnelli 7
airports
  Florence 221, 233
  Pisa 220, 232
Aldous Huxley 119, 142
antiques fairs
  Arezzo 118
  Cortona 125
Apuan Alps 152
Archivo Alinari 62
Arezzo 117, 118, 119
Arno 17, 18, 23, 43, 130, 137
Assisi 11, 160, 168

B

Bardi Chapel 34, 61
Barga 155
Bargello 20, 32, 39, 46
Barrett Browning, Elizabeth 70
bars, general 227
Bartolo 97, 122
Basilica della Porziuncola 168
Basilica di S.Maria degli
  Angeli 169
Basilica di Santa Chiara 168
Basilica di San Francesco,
  Arezzo 118
Basilica di San Francesco,
  Assisi 160, 165
beaches 143, 148
  Forte dei Marmi 142
  Viareggio 143
Bicci di Lorenzo 117
boat building, Viareggio 145
boat charter 145
Boboli Gardens 47, 64
Bonsai Gardens 65
Botticelli 48, 53, 114, 119
Brancacci Chapel 33, 37, 60
breakdowns 224

Browning, Robert 71
Brunelleschi 26, 28, 30, 32-34,
  37, 47, 57, 60-61, 102, 117
bus travel 149, 221

C

Caiano 63
Camaiore 152
Campo dei Miracoli 135
Canadian Island 65
Canova 47
Carrara 39, 57, 104, 154-155
car hire 222
Casa di Dante 24, 62
Castellina in Chianti 120
Cellini 18, 20
Certaldo 121
Chapel of Santa Fina 97
Charles Dickens 72
chemists 230
Chianti 196, 197
Chianti vineyards 197-200
Chiesa Nuova 168
cigarettes 228
Cimabue 25, 61
Collegiata, San Gimignano 97
Colle di Val D'Elsa 121
Contrada 85, 87
Cortona 124, 126
credit card, lost, stolen 231

D

Dante 24, 25, 62
David 18, 20, 37, 39, 41-43, 46, 142
David and Goliath 41
da Vinci, Leonardo 30, 102, 114,
  121, 155
Dickens, Charles 72
directory enquiries 228
Dominican 34, 58, 60
Donatello 18, 28, 30, 33, 34, 37-38,
  46, 57, 61, 114, 117
driving 222-224
Duomo 134
  Lucca (di San Martino) 104
  Siena 90
  Florence (Santa Maria del

Fiore) 25-26, 28, 30, 37, 53, 58
Baptistry 26, 28
Campanile (Bell Tower) 25-26, 28, 134

E

Eremo delle Carceri 168
Etruria 10
Etruscan 10, 62, 98, 121, 126, 130

F

Ferragamo 7, 19, 75
Florence 12, 18-77
Florin 18
Forte dei Marmi 142, 144, 148-149
Francis 162-164
Fra Angelico 59, 125
Fresco technique 34

G

Gaiolo in Chianti 120
Galileo 61, 63, 131-133
Galleria dell'Accademia 42
gardens
  Apuan Alps 153
  Florence
    Boboli Gardens 47, 64
    Bonsai Gardens 65
    Giardino dei Semplici 65
  Lucca 106, 107
  Pisa
    Orto Botanico 131
Ghibelline 11, 83
Ghiberti 28, 30, 32-33, 37
Ghirlandaio 34, 38, 60, 97, 104
Giambologna 18, 20
Giardino Botanico, Lucca 106
Giardino dei Semplici 65
Gino Severini 124
Giotto 25, 28, 46, 165, 168
Giro D'Italia 144
Gondi Chapel 34
Grand Tour 68-69
Greve in Chianti 120
Gucci 74, 75

Guelph 11, 24, 50, 83, 96, 124
Guinigi 103, 105

H

Hardy, Thomas 73
horse riding 148

J

Jacopo della Quercia 97, 104
John the Baptist 18, 28, 46, 60

L

Lake Trasimeno 126-127
Leaning Tower 135
Le Cascine 65
Lippi 33, 60, 104
Loggia dei Lanzi 20
Lombards 10
Lucca 30, 102-111, 153

M

Machiavelli 20, 22, 61, 115
Masaccio 18, 30, 33, 37, 60, 117
Masolino 33
Matteo Civitali 104
medical treatment 229, 230
Medici 11-12, 20, 38, 47, 48, 50-58, 63, 122, 124, 131
Michelangelo 12, 18, 21, 32, 34, 38-43, 46, 53, 57, 60, 61, 116, 118, 142, 155
Montalcino 122
Montepulciano 122
Monteriggioni 121
motorways 223
Museo Archeologico 62, 118
Museo Civico, Sanselpocro 119
Museo dell'Opera del Duomo 28
Museo Diocesano, Cortona 125
Museo di Basilica di S. Maria Degli Angeli 169
Museo di Firenze ComíEra 62
Museo di Storia della Scienza 63
Museo Horne 63

Museo Nazionale di Villa
  Guinigi 103
museums & churches,
  general 227
Museum of Sacred Art, San
Gimignano 97

O

Orto Botanico 131
Ospedale di Santa Maria della
  Scala 90

P

Palazzo dei Guinigi 105
Palazzo del Popolo 98
Palazzo Pfanner 105
Palazzo Pitti 20, 47
Palazzo Rucellai 62
Palazzo Vecchio 20-21, 23, 47
Palio 82-87
Parco Naturale delle Alpi
  Apuane 153
Passeggiata 6, 102
Passignano 127
Pazzi Chapel 30, 61
Petraia 63
Piazzale Michelangelo 18, 42, 43
Piazza della Signoria 12, 20
Piazza del Campo 82, 86
Pienza 123
Piero della Francesca 117, 119
Pietrasanta 57, 142, 148
Pietro Pellegrini 153
Pieve 152
Pisa 128-139
Pisano family 28, 32, 134-137
Pisan June 137
Pisa airport 220, 232, 233
Pisa University 131
Piscina Nannini 65
Pitti Palace 23, 47, 64
police 231
Ponte Vecchio 20, 22, 23, 77
Porta San Nicolo 43
postage 228
Prada 75, 142

Puccini 108-109

R

Radda in Chianti 120
Raphael 47
Renaissance 10, 12, 18, 25, 28, 51,
  53, 106, 115, 117
restaurants
  Arrezo 184
  Bagni di Lucca 184
  Camaiore 184
  Carrara 184
  Castellina in Chianti 185
  Castelnuovo di Garfagnana 185
  Colle val d'Elsa 185
  Cortona 186
  Florence 174, 176-179, 180-183
  Forte dei Marmi 187
  Greve in Chianti 188
  Lucca 188
  Massa Pisana 188
  Montecatani Terme 189
  Montefollonico 189
  Montepulciano 189
  Pescia 190
  Pienza 190
  Pietrasanta 191
  Pisa 136, 191
  Poggibonsi 191
  Sanselpolcro 193
  San Gimignano 192
  San Vincenzo 193
  Siena 194
  Viareggio 195
Reubens 47
Robert Browning 71
Rocca Maggiore 168
rollerblading 148

S

Sanselpocro 117, 119
Santa Croce 30, 34, 61, 76-77
Santa Maria della Spina, Pisa 137
Santa Maria del Carmine 33, 37,
  60, 179

Basilica Santa Maria del
  Carmine 33
Brancacci Chapel 33, 37, 60
Santa Maria del Fiore 26, 58
Santa Maria Novella 25, 30, 33,
  34, 60, 63, 77, 133, 207, 220
San Gimignano 11, 96, 97, 98, 99
San Lorenzo Basilica 57
San Marco 58, 59, 65
San Michele In Foro, Lucca 104
San Miniato 43, 60
San Spirito 60
Savonarola, Girolamo 20, 58, 59
self-catering 225, 226
Seravezza 155
shopping
  Arezzo 208
  Colle di Val D'Elsa 208
  designer outlet 75, 208
  Florence 75, 76, 77, 206, 207
  Gaiole in Chianti 208
  Greve in Chianti 209
  Lucca 105
  Montecatini Terme 209
  Montepulciano 210
  Pienza 211
  Pisa 211
  Radda in Chianti 212
  San Gimignano 99, 213
  Siena 213
Siena 11, 43, 55, 80-93, 131
Siena Cathedral 90
Spedale degli Innocenti 30
speed limits 223
St Dominic 58
St Francis 11, 58, 160-165, 169
supermarkets 149, 228, 229
Superstrada 43
swimming pools 225
  Piscina Nannini 65

T

Taddeo Gaddi 61
Tintoretto 104
tipping 228
Titian 47

Tornabuoni Chapel 34
Torre del Guinigi 103
Torre del Lago 108, 109
train travel 221
Treasury of the Basilica, Perkins
  collection 168
Tuscan cuisine 172-175

U

Uccello, Paolo 26
Uffizi Gallery 20, 48

V

Versace 7
Viareggio 108, 143, 144-145,
  148-149
villas 225, 226
Villa di Poggio 63, 108
Villa Garzoni, Lucca 106
Villa Mansi, Lucca 107
Villa Pecci-Blunt, Lucca 107
Villa Torrigiani, Lucca 107
vineyards 198
  Florence region 199
  Gaiole in Chianti 199
  Greve in Chianti 200
  Lucca 203
  Montalcino 201
  Montepulciano 202
  Radda in Chianti 200
  Siena 203
Volterra 121

Author's Favourites

When I was a teenager, I didn't like to read. I found it boring because it took too long to read a whole book. Then I borrowed a book on speed reading from the library and taught myself. Now I always have a large stack of books by my bedside which regularly collapses into what my husband calls 'Hope's heap'.

These are some of the books that have been part of the heap while writing this book.

W. Somerset Maugham
Then and Now
Niccolo Machiavelli has been sent to Imola to negotiate with Cesare Borgia. There he lusts after the young married Aurelia and plots to sleep with her. But who is behind the counter-plot to prevent him?

W. Somerset Maugham
Up at the Villa
A proper Englishwoman commits a crime of passion at her villa in Florence. In desperation, she enlists the aid of the cad in her social circle to dispose of the body.

Sarah Dunant
The Birth of Venus
Interesting twist on a coming of age story set in Florence during the years of Giacomo Savonarala.

Frances Mayes
Under the Tuscan Sun
Bella Tuscany
In Tuscany
Under the Tuscan Sun is the best of the ex-pat property restoration books set in Tuscany and is also a film. The story is getting thin in *Bella Tuscany* which is filled out with recipes.

Paul Gervais
A Garden in Lucca
An American couple (two men) buy a villa in Lucca and restore the garden. It is the author's honest passion in wanting to know everything about Italian gardens that catches the reader's attention.

Lisa St Aubin de Teran
A Valley in Italy
The valley is actually in Umbria but this most whimsical of the house restoration memoirs has a light-hearted charm. This book is peopled with interesting characters: her teenage daughter is especially endearing.

The Oxford Book of
Travel Verse
A superb collection of poetry about travel. The book is separated by destination and includes Shelley, Keats, Byron and the Brownings, together with Day-Lewis, Dylan Thomas and other poets.

Essential Shopping Italian

English	Italian	Pronunciation
Open	**Aperto**	*ah-***pehr**-*toh*
Closed	**Chiuso**	*kee-***oo**-*soh*
How much is this?	**Quanto costa questo?**	**kwan**-*toh* **koh**-*sta* **kwes**-*toh?*
Can you write down the price?	**Puo scrivere il prezzo?**	*pwo skree-***veh**-*reh* *eel* **preh**-*tso?*
Do you take credit cards?	**Prendete carte di credito?**	*pren-***deh**-*teh* **kar**-*teh dee* **kreh**-*dee-toh?*
I'd like to buy . . .	**Vorrei comprare . . .**	*voh-***ray** *kom-***prah**-*reh*
Do you have anything . . .?	**Avete qualcosa . . .?**	*ah-***veh**-*teh* *kwahl-***koh**-*sah*
larger	**piu grande**	*pyoo* **grahn**-*deh*
smaller	**piu piccolo**	*pyoo* **pee**-*kohl-oh*
Do you have any others?	**Ne avete altri?**	*neh ah-***veh**-*teh* **ahl**-*tree*
I'm just looking.	**Sto solo guardando.**	*sto* **soh**-*loh gwar-***dan**-*doh*

Size Chart

Women's dresses, coats and skirts

Italian	40	42	44	46	48	50	52
British	8	10	12	14	16	18	20
American	6	8	10	12	14	16	18

Women's shoes

Italian	36	37	38	39	40	41
British	3	4	5	6	7	8
American	5	6	7	8	9	10

Men's suits

Italian	44	46	48	50	52	54	56	58 (size)
British	34	36	38	40	42	44	46	48 (inches)
American	34	36	38	40	42	44	46	48 (inches)

Men's shirts (collar size)

Italian	36	38	39	41	42	44	46	48 (cm)
British	14	15	15½	16	16½	17	17½	18 (inches)
American	14	15	15½	16	16½	17	17½	18 (inches)

Men's shoes

Italian	39	40	41	42	43	44	45	46
British	6	7	7½	8	9	10	11	12
American	7	7½	8	8½	9½	10½	11	11½

Your first port of call
for all things Italian...

· Our new titles available for purchase online.
· Regular updates on restaurants and shopping
· Links to the best sites for wine, food and travel info

www.purpleguide.com

email:info@purpleguide.com